On Interpretation

A Critical Analysis

ANNETTE BARNES

D1500370

Basil Blackwell

First published 1988

Basil Blackwell Ltd
108 Cowley Road, Oxford, OX4 1JF, UK

Basil Blackwell Inc.
432 Park Avenue South, Suite 1503
New York, NY 10016, USA

British Library Cataloguing in Publication Data

Barnes, Annette
    On interpretation: a critical analysis
    1. Philosophy
    I. Title
    700'.1   NX640

    ISBN 0–631–15947–9
    ISBN 0–631–15963–0 Pbk

Typeset in 10 on 12 pt Sabon
by Cambrian Typesetters, Frimley, Surrey
Printed in Great Britain by
Page Bros. (Norwich) Ltd.

Contents

Acknowledgements

I want to thank Gerald Barnes and G. A. Cohen for their extremely generous, insightful and always helpful criticism, and the National Endowment for the Humanities for a year's fellowship to work on this book.

I am grateful to the Editor of *The Journal of Aesthetics and Art Criticism* for permission to reprint some material in chapter 2 that originally appeared in this journal.

1

Introduction

In this philosophical study of interpretation I focus primarily, although not exclusively, on the interpeting done, and the interpretations given, by critics in the arts. While critics readily offer what they consider to be interpretations, there is no consensus, among either critics or philosophers, about what interpretation is. This lack of consensus exists, I should like to think, despite rather than because of the fact that philosophers and others have written extensively about critical interpretation in an attempt to characterize the relevant concept or concepts.

My general aim is to provide an account of interpretation which explains how two significant features of critical practice can coexist – how critical practice *both* tolerates a plurality of sometimes incompatible interpretations of artworks *and* nevertheless allows that confrontation and significant defeat may take place between critics. In contrast, many of the well-known accounts of interpretation fail to do justice to these two features. There is a tendency for those who accept multiple interpretations to deny confrontation and significant defeat, and for those who affirm confrontation and significant defeat to reject multiplicity.

For example, a number of theorists who argue for criticism's tolerance of multiple interpretations for a single work construe interpretive remarks in such a way that seemingly incompatible interpretations for the work turn out not to be genuinely incompatible.[1] These seemingly incompatible interpretations, it is held, can be altogether equally acceptable, each can satisfy whatever requirements an interpretation must satisfy; critics who advance them do not in fact directly challenge or defeat one another. A number of other theorists construe interpretive remarks as ordinary statements and argue against the legitimacy of critical tolerance.[2] On their account critics offer genuinely incompatible interpretations, and thereby directly challenge and, not infrequently, defeat interpretations incompatible with their own.

Both those who argue for tolerance and the absence of defeat of any interesting kind and those who argue for defeat and the absence of tolerance share the error of supposing that if incompatible interpretations are tolerable, significant defeat is impossible. I argue that it is possible for criticism legitimately to tolerate incompatible (*genuinely* and not seemingly incompatible) interpretations for a single work and for critics to directly challenge and defeat other critics.

While I am not alone in trying to reconcile multiplicity and significant defeat,[3] my position differs from others in the particular way that I seek to effect this reconciliation. I argue that the kind of defeat that is typical in criticism is not what it is frequently assumed to be; for critics do not typically defeat other critics by showing what they say to be false. Rather, the prevalent mode of defeat is defeat by a 'relevant counter-possibility', a defeat which I show is compatible with multiplicity.

Defeat by a relevant counterpossibility is available for interpretive remarks only if these remarks have a certain status – that of ordinary statements. In a good deal of recent theorizing about interpretation this status has been explicitly denied. It is argued that, given what meanings are, given what texts are, given what art works are . . . interpretative remarks cannot be statements taking the values 'true' and 'false'. I show why these current arguments do not prove that interpretive remarks are not statements. But while I argue that many interpretive remarks should be viewed as statements, this does not imply that *all* should be. I discuss circumstances in which an interpretive remark may have a different status.

If, as I claim, the supposition that interpretive remarks are statements does justice to important features of critical practice and allows us to explain – without ruling out multiple interpretations – how critics can confront and significantly defeat one another, does this supposition allow us to distinguish interpreting from describing? I argue that we can indeed distinguish between them although the various conditions that have looked promising either as individually necessary or as individually sufficient for one or the other activity are not in fact so.

If my account of interpretation is correct, then rationality and objectivity are possible in interpretive criticism. An aim of the book is to show what this rationality and objectivity consist in. In the course of my discussion I criticize some widely misused contrasts, which I believe help to obscure what is needed for rationality and objectivity, and I sketch more acceptable alternatives to them.

If the alternatives I describe are correct, then one need not choose in interpretive criticism between attending to artistic intention and disregarding it, between treating critical remarks as discovering properties and treating them as imputing properties, between applying 'true' and 'false' to all interpretive remarks and applying them to none. On my account, while the interpretive task is inherently not completable, works do have determinate meanings; truth has a place in interpretive criticism, even though that place is limited; and interpretations are often statements, even though they need not always be.

I begin my discussion of interpretation in chapter 2 by considering the logical conditions of interpretation – whether, for example, critics who interpret must be in a special epistemic position *vis-à-vis* their objects, and, in particular, whether they must be ignorant of, or puzzled about, some aspect of the artwork. If, for example, it were obvious to a critic that the figure in Manet's *Olympia* is a woman, could the critic be interpreting the figure as a woman? I establish links between interpretating, the obvious, and the known, links which I believe hold generally, that is, which apply to interpreting in all domains.

Next, in chapter 3, I consider and reject a number of possible objections to the theses developed so far. I show, for example, how the claims I have defended in chapter 2 can be made independent of a standard of acceptability for an interpretation.

In chapters 4 through 7 I discuss the status of critical interpretations and the standard of acceptability for them. I approach these questions by considering whether interpretive remarks are defeasible, and if they are, how they are.

Chapter 4 considers whether interpretive remarks *can* be statements taking the values 'true' and 'false'. I discuss an argument given by Joseph Margolis which denies them this status and acceptability standard. I establish a link between successfully executed artistic intention and an interpretation's truth, being careful to distinguish this link from the stronger one demanded by the intentionalist. The truth of an interpretation is distinguished from its acceptability. I show the latter to be logically independent of the former.

In chapter 5 I extend my criticism of the argument discussed in chapter 4, offering more satisfactory accounts of discovery, of the nature of artworks, and of ways of handling incompatible interpretations. I also consider and reject an argument given by Robert Matthews which purports to establish that interpretive remarks are not as a *matter of fact* statements.

I claim in chapter 6 that one can plausibly construe two well-known theories about interpretation, the theories of Stanley Fish and Jacques Derrida, as offering arguments against the significant defeasibility of interpretive remarks. These arguments, I claim, do not succeed in establishing that interpretive remarks are not significantly defeasible.

Chapter 7 presents a detailed account of the kinds of defeasibility which could be appropriate to interpretive remarks if they had the status of statements, of hypotheses, of reports of special types of experiences, or of prescriptions.[4] I then look to critical practice to see which, if any, of the kinds of defeasibility are appropriate to actual critical interpretations. I show that only one kind of status, that of statement, allows for defeat of a certain kind – defeat by a 'relevant counterpossibility' – and I argue that this kind of defeat is common in art criticism.

Next, in chapter 8, I consider whether, if interpretive remarks are statements, one can distinguish between interpreting and describing. While I argue that one can so distinguish, all that is available for doing so are sets of conditions each of which is sufficient for one or the other activity, although no one of them is necessary.

I end my discussion in chapter 9 by considering the scope of critical interpretation, whether all artworks are suitable objects of interpretation, and whether interpreting is irreducibly pluralistic, a set of diverse activities rather than a single activity with diverse objects.

Finally, a few additional words about the structure and method of the book. In chapters 2 and 3, and again in 7 and 8, I set forth my own major theses, and in consequence these chapters are written with fully detailed articulation. In chapters 4 through 6 my aim is different, and so accordingly is my method. The object of these chapters is to disarm opponents; and, while I use the enterprise to advance positive positions on some further issues of critical interpretation, there is less need in this context for the rigorous method and the formal style of the other chapters. Chapter 1, the present chapter, is introductory, and chapter 9 rounds off the discussion.

In discussions about critical interpretation, speaking precisely is not often enough the practice. I have tried throughout to be conceptually rigorous without being unduly technical, to be scrupulous with regard to significant detail. Those accustomed to the luxuriance of suggestibility might find portions of my text sobering, those dismissive of a particular kind of theorizing might find it over scrupulous. I address myself to the reader who, puzzled by critical interpretation and confronted with dichotomies thought to be both mutually exclusive and mutually exhaustive, is satisfied with neither of the alternatives.

Notes

1 Stanley Fish, Jacques Derrida, Joseph Margolis, Charles Stevenson and Roger Scruton, for example, construe interpretations as other than statements taking the values 'true' and 'false'.

2 Monroe Beardsley was a leading advocate of this position. A number of practicing critics also hold this view.

3 Nelson Goodman, for example, argues for multiple *right* interpretations.

4 I identify, for example, Monroe Beardsley with the view that interpretive remarks are statements (cf. *Aesthetics* (2nd edn) Indianapolis, 1981), p. 9, 'a critical interpretation, for the purpose of this book, is a statement that purports to declare the "meaning" of a work of art'.); Joseph Margolis, *Art & Philosophy* (Atlantic Highlands, 1980), with the view that they are hypotheses; Charles

Stevenson, 'Interpretation and evaluation in aesthetics', in William Kennick ed., *Art and Philosophy* (1st edn; New York, 1964), 466–97, with the view that they are prescriptions. That they are reports of special types of experiences is suggested by what Roger Scruton says in *Art and Imagination* (London, 1974).

2

Interpreting, the Obvious and the Known Part I

When critics interpret works of art they do something. I want to consider, among these cases of interpreting, those in which the results of whatever is done are given to us in words. It seems uncontentious and perhaps not very informative to say that in such cases the critics are trying to understand the work. And it is clear that whenever anyone is trying to understand something, one is thinking about that something. So, to interpret, as Wittgenstein said, is to think.[1] But obviously not all thinking is interpreting. What kind of thinking about a work of art is to be identified with interpreting that work?

If I think, concerning a literary work, that it has one thousand pages, is long, is shorter than the *Oxford English Dictionary*, then although I am thinking about the work, I would not ordinarily be said to be interpreting it. I may not even be thinking about it as a literary work. Suppose, however, that I think, concerning a work, that it is enigmatic, or ironic, or that one of its characters is avoiding love. It is more likely that I am interpreting here. What am I doing in the one case that I am not doing in the other?

The answer can't be classifying, for in either case I do that, using words to effect the classification. In either case the object in question is included in the extension of a predicate, whether the predicate is 'long', 'shorter than the *OED*', 'ironic', or 'has a character who is avoiding love'. The object so labelled is associated with any other objects to which the predicate also applies. To interpret is, in this sense of classifying, to classify, but since not all classifying appears to be interpreting, the question becomes – what kind of classifying of a work of art is to be identified with interpreting it?

One philosopher has suggested, as a step toward an answer, that a critic's classifying of the obvious in works of art does not count as interpreting. If a work, for example, were obviously ironic, then on this hypothesis, it would follow that a critic would not be interpreting if he[2] labelled the work ironic. Is it the case, then, that when one sorts things using labels that obviously fit them one is not interpreting them?

Interpreting and the obvious

What is it for something to be obvious? What is obvious to one critic is not always obvious to another. 'Obvious' is a relative term: 'It's obvious' can always be countered by 'To whom?'. Moreover, if a given critic believes that something is obvious, for example, that a character is avoiding love, it does not seem to follow that the critic is not interpreting when he speaks of the character in this way. It seems possible that he believes it to be obvious because he has interpreted the character in just this way. Nevertheless, as William Kennick has observed, it does seem initially plausible to think that the obvious does count in some way against interpreting.

> To say that Manet's *Olympia* contains a nude woman is to describe that picture, in part, but not to interpret it. So also for saying that the atmosphere of a Dutch interior, for example, a typical Pieter de Hooch, is quiet and peaceful. Anyone can see this at a glance, which suggests that statements about the obvious in a work of art, for example, that the first phrase of Herrick's 'Corinna's Going A-Maying' is 'Get up', are to be classified as descriptions and not as interpretations.[3]

If it is obvious that the figure in *Olympia* is a woman, there seems to be no room for interpreting the figure as a woman. But if there were no room in these cases for interpreting, how could it be correct to say of the critic who believes it obvious that a character is avoiding love that he is interpreting?

Is obvious and seems obvious

A distinction needs to be drawn here between something being obvious and something seeming obvious. When it *is* obvious, for example, that the figure in *Olympia* is a woman, it follows that the figure in *Olympia* is a woman. When it *seems* obvious that the figure is a woman, it does not follow that the figure is a woman, for what seems obvious may not in fact be obvious. Although this distinction is often glossed over in ordinary language, it needs to be kept clearly in mind if the connection between the obvious and interpreting is to be understood.

Although one's claim that something is obvious often takes the form, 'it is obvious that . . .', or 'it is obvious to me that . . .', if it turns out that what is believed obvious is not the case, then one was only entitled to a weaker locution, viz., 'it seems obvious that . . .', or 'it seems obvious to me that . . . '. It is true that when one has what one considers sufficient warrant for one's beliefs, one may find the 'seems obvious' form inappropriate, for this form can suggest some measure of doubt. However, given that one's beliefs may be mistaken, no matter how firm one's conviction about them, what a person believed obvious may turn out not to have been obvious, because it was not true. For example, although many ordinary people in the tenth century believed it to be obvious that the earth was flat, given that the earth was spherical, it could not have been obvious that it was flat. Similarly, although a critic may say that it is obvious that a character is avoiding love, if it were to turn out that the character was not avoiding love, then it could not have been obvious that he was avoiding it.[4]

Nevertheless, this is not to say that something's being obvious to me is simply a matter of its seeming obvious to me plus its being true. For example, suppose I know that Hilary, one of my guests at dinner, had a Picasso with which she vowed never to part. It seems obvious to me that someone at my dinner has a Picasso. It happens, however, that Hilary's escort, Craig, who is also my dinner guest, has a Picasso, although Hilary no longer does. While a great many people know of Craig's Picasso, I do not. Here it seems obvious to me that someone at my dinner has a Picasso, and it is true and obvious in general that someone at my dinner has one. Nevertheless, it is not obvious to me that someone at my dinner has a Picasso.

Is it the case that a person to whom something is obvious is not interpreting? That is, is the following claim correct?

> (I) If it is obvious to a person that x is F (the figure in the painting is a woman, the novel is long), then that person is not interpreting x as F (the figure in the painting as a woman, the novel as long).

Suppose it is not initially obvious to a critic that a character in a play has three daughters. The critic has to weigh one remark which suggests to him a fourth daughter against all others that do not. In these circumstances it seems that the critic could be interpreting the character as having three daughters. But suppose that the critic has simply misread the one remark, and that his mistake is pointed out to him. It becomes obvious to him, as it is to others, that the character has three daughters. Would he be interpreting the character as having three daughters once this is obvious to him? Although it is possible to interpret if one doesn't find something obvious, once something not merely *seems*, but *is* obvious to one, interpreting seems to be blocked.

But is my interpreting always blocked in the face of the obvious to me, and if it were, what would account for this? If it is not always blocked, why, in at least many cases, does it seem to be?

Wittgenstein said that 'it is easy to recognize cases in which we are *interpreting*. When we interpret we form hypotheses, which may prove false.'[5] It seems to me that a plausible way of understanding Wittgenstein's talk of a person's hypothesis proving false here is in terms of what I shall call the epistemic possibility of being mistaken about a hypothesis. My hypothesis may prove false just in case it is epistemically possible for me to be mistaken about it. I shall use the notion of epistemic possibility as an unanalyzed primitive notion. I intend it to correspond in sense to such comparatively natural expressions as 'as far as I know, it is possible that . . .', 'given what I know, it is possible that . . .', and 'on the basis of what I know, it is possible that . . .'.

According to the proposed understanding of Wittgenstein's remark, it is sometimes *not* the case, when I form a hypothesis (or, perhaps, judgement), that my hypothesis (or judgement) may prove false. This is not to say that there are cases in which I am, or regard myself as being, infallible. Nor is it to say simply that I sometimes form hypotheses which are true, although the truth of my hypothesis is a necessary *part* of any case in which it is not possible for my hypothesis to prove false. It is to make the more complex claim that sometimes, given what I know, there is no possibility of my being mistaken about my hypothesis, i.e., that sometimes, when I form a hypothesis, it is not epistemically possible for me to be mistaken about it. A full analysis of the claim that such-and-such is or is not epistemically possible would no doubt reveal much of interest, but to pursue that analysis at this point would be to digress too widely from the present argument.

Given this way of understanding Wittgenstein, his remark – 'when we interpret we form hypotheses, which may prove false' – suggests that unless it were epistemically possible for the person to be mistaken about his hypothesis, viz., mistaken about whether x is F, that person could not interpret x as F. If this were the case, then one could explain why its being obvious to him that x is F counts against interpreting. The explanation might go as follows.

When it is obvious to a person that x is F – for example, when it is obvious to a person that the figure in *Olympia* is a woman – that person not only sees that the figure in *Olympia* is a woman, but knows that the figure is a woman. Moreover, in such a case the person also knows that he knows this. If it is (versus merely seems) obvious to you, the reader, that this book is written in English, then you know that this book is written in English, and you know that you know this.

But if one knows that the figure in *Olympia* is a woman, and one also knows that one knows it, then it is not epistemically possible for one to be mistaken about whether the figure in *Olympia* is a woman, for it to be false that the figure in *Olympia* is a woman. But if it is not epistemically possible for one to be mistaken about whether the figure in *Olympia* is a woman, then one would have satisfied a condition sufficient for not interpreting. So runs the explanation of why its being obvious to one that x is F counts against interpreting.

The argument in simplified form is this:

(1) If it is obvious to A that x is F, then A knows that x is F and A knows that he knows this.

(2) When A knows that x is F, and A knows that he knows this, then it is not epistemically possible for A to be mistaken about x being F.

(3) Unless it is epistemically possible for A to be mistaken about x being F, A cannot interpret x as F.

Therefore,

(4) If it is obvious to A that x is F, then A is not interpreting x as F.

In order to avoid the objection against (2) that I can know that x is F at time t_1, while it is still epistemically possible for me to be mistaken about x being F because, for example, I can forget that x is F by t_2, or not believe that x is F at t_2, the entire argument is to be understood as relativized to a single arbitrary time t.

It is important to notice that when A believes that x is F and A's belief is correct, although it is, so to speak, not then metaphysically possible for A to be mistaken about x being F, this can be, nevertheless, epistemically possible. It can be the case that as far as one knows, the hypothesis that x is F may be false, even though one correctly believes that it is not. However, when one knows that one knows that x is F, then it is not even epistemically possible for one to be mistaken about x being F: it is not the case that one's hypothesis that x is F may prove false.[6]

Something like this way of arguing may be what Kennick himself had in mind when he suggested that the obvious tells against interpreting. Kennick asks whether, if Piero della Francesca had told someone that the egg in his *Madonna and Saints* was an ostrich egg and what it symbolized, he would have been interpreting his own picture. There is no question that when art historian Millard Meiss argues that it is an ostrich egg, rather than the chicken egg it may obviously seem, he is interpreting. Or, Kennick asks, when Jesus explains the Parable of the Tares to his disciples at their request, as reported in the Gospel according to St Matthew, does he interpret the parable? To Kennick 'it seems clear' that if one of the disciples had given the same explanation in the same words, it would be an interpretation. 'Can the same words', he asks, 'although uttered by different persons, both be and not be an interpretation? If so, are Jesus' words not an interpretation of the parable because he could not have been mistaken about what it meant, or about what he meant by it; could not have got it wrong?'[7] (The assumption here is that lying, deception, and misleading have been ruled out.) Kennick's remarks are tentative, put in the form of questions and suggestions. Whether these suggestions hold up depends upon whether an argument like the one outlined above is sound.

I have already discussed premises (1) and (2). Let us turn to premise (3).

In 'Describing and interpreting a work of art',[8] Robert Matthews presents a tempting view which, if correct, would provide support for this premise. Although Matthews' view is ultimately unsatisfactory,[9] it is instructive to examine it initially.

Matthews attempts to provide a new way of distinguishing between describing and interpreting. While he regards both as speech acts, they differ from one another in what he calls their 'epistemic basis'. In interpreting one is in a weaker epistemic position *vis à vis* the object than in describing. Whereas in describing the person must be in a position to know whether the statements constituting his description are true of the object, in interpreting the person must not be in a position to know this, but must be in a position to know 'that the statements constituting his interpretation are plausible, reasonable, or at least defensible on evidence provided by the interpretandum'.[10] Whereas in a description a speaker 'conversationally implicates that he knows that p',[11] in an interpretation a speaker only conversationally implicates plausibility or defensibility, he implicates some doubt.

If Matthews were right, then when one is interpreting x as F, one cannot be in a position to know whether x is F and, hence, one cannot know tht x is F. But if one does not know that x is F, then it would be epistemically possible for one to be mistaken about x being F, possible for it to prove false that x is F. So, on Matthews' account, in any interpreting, the condition that premise (3) posits as necessary must indeed always be satisifed.

It is true that on Matthews' account this condition could also be satisfied if one were describing – in describing, the person is required only to be in a position to know whether *x* is *F*, not to know that *x* is *F* – but he would deny that the satisfaction of this condition was necessary for describing. If one is incorrectly describing *x*, it is epistemically possible for one to be mistaken about *x* being *F*. If, however, one is in a position to know, and does know *x* to be *F*, and knows that one does, then it is not epistemically possible for one to be mistaken about *x* being *F*, although one could be describing *x* as *F*. Has Matthews shown, then, that premise (3) is true?

In a response to Matthews, Michael Hancher has in effect argued that this does not follow. Although Hancher's specific target is to show that being in a position to know does not rule out interpreting, and although examples which show this need not also show that knowing, when one knows that one knows, does not rule out interpreting, nevertheless, some of the examples he uses will, if genuine counter-examples, serve to show the inadequacy of both views.

> When the editors of *The Norton Anthology of English Literature* gloss 'Lycidas', line 109, 'The pilot of the Galilean lake', as a reference to St. Peter, they are interpreting the line for the reader (it would be odd to say that they are 'describing' the line, or even the meaning of the line) . . . In this case, at least, they know (and, *a fortiori*, are 'in a position to know') whereof they speak.

> If I am having trouble understanding a passage in my calculus textbook, I may go to you and ask, 'Would you interpret this for me?' . . . Certainly I would *not* put such a request only if I believed that you were '*not* in a position to know whether the statements constituting [your] interpretation' of the passage were true! Much the same is true of foreign-language interpretation in general. [12]

The last example he gives is that of final judicial interpretations of legal documents. Supreme court judges, he points out, are in a stronger epistemic position than plausibility with regard to their interpretations, for here ' "saying" actually "makes it so" '. [13]

Other examples come to mind. Imagine Wittgenstein's example

of an illustration appearing in several places in a textbook. 'Each time the text supplies the interpretation of the illustration', for example, 'here a glass cube, there an inverted open box, there a wire frame of that shape, there three boards forming a solid angle'.[14] Suppose you know what the illustration represents in each instance, since you have read the book. Aren't you giving the appropriate interpretation each time you correctly say when asked – that's a glass cube?

Or to use an example suggested by Matthews. You interpret a friend's sudden coldness as a sign of irritation. Now suppose I speak to your friend and he tells me that he wasn't irritated with you but was preoccupied with family problems. Moreover, he is telling the truth. If I then tell you that you've misinterpreted his behavior, that it should be interpreted in the following way: . . . , am I not interpreting his behavior for you?

These examples, if correct, would seem to show that premise (3) is false, for they show that even when a person knows that x is F (in these cases we are also assuming that the person knows himself to know this) and, therefore, it is not epistemically possible for him to be mistaken about x being F, that person can be interpreting. Let us look more closely at them.

Consider judicial interpretations of legal documents. The interpreters in these cases are in a special position with regard to x being F. As Hancher acknowledges, their interpretations are 'beyond the reach of any truth-test'. When, for example, the Supreme Court justices ruled that the hostage agreement worked out by the Carter Administration with Iran was legal, they knew that the hostage agreement, thenceforth, would be legal. Before the time they declared it legal there was room for mistake about, for example, such matters as the nature of the relevant precedents, and hence they did not then yet know it to be legal. If no clear direction was given by precedent (e.g., there were none, or conflicting ones, etc.), they would not while deliberating know that the agreement was legal, for no right of way of viewing the agreement would exist prior to their deciding upon a way. However, what leaves premise (3) unscathed by these cases is the fact that the interpreters *must have finished* interpreting *before* they can *know* x to be F. While these cases, so regarded, do not challenge premise (3), whether they serve Hancher's purpose against Matthews is another matter, one I shall not deal with.

The other examples cited present a different problem. When a person interprets x as F for another – what the calculus passage, a friend's behavior, a figure in a text, or a sentence from a foreign language means – he can, as Hancher points out, know that x is F, and know that he does. If interpreting for another is a form of interpreting, as it seems clearly to be, then premise (3) is false.

Interpreting for oneself and interpreting for others

Suppose we try to deal with this by restricting premise (3), excluding interpreting for another from it. Hancher acknowledges that 'though I might ask you to "interpret" the hard calculus passage for me, . . . you would be unlikely, at the time, to say to me "*I interpret* the passage this way: . . ." – unless you were in some doubt as to its meaning, . . . the use of the explicit performative formula "I interpret x as p" may indeed implicate some doubt, as Matthews suggests.'[15]

Let us understand premise (3) in the following way:

(3r) Unless it is epistemically possible for A to be mistaken about x being F, A cannot interpret x as F for himself.

What (3r) does not rule out is the possibility of interpreting for another even when it is not epistemically possible for one to be mistaken about x is F. Given this reading of (3), the conclusion (4) becomes:

(4r) If it is obvious to A that x is F, then A is not interpreting x as F for himself.

If (4r) were true, would this show that (I) – if it is obvious to a person that x is F, then that person is not interpreting x as F – was true?

Is (I) true? If interpreting x as F in (I) includes interpreting x as F for another, then (I) is clearly false. It may be obvious to me what a sentence in English means in a context, although I may have to interpret the sentence for a non-English speaker. If we exclude interpreting x as F for another, then if (4r) is true, the following restricted version of (I) must be true.

(Ir) If it is obvious to a person that x is F, then that person is not interpreting x as F for himself.

(Ir) and (4r) are equivalent.

A person might fail to see the impossibility of interpreting x as F for oneself when it is obvious to one that x is F, if he does not keep in mind the distinction between something's *seeming* obvious to one and its *being* obvious to one (and hence the distinction between believing that x is F and knowing that x is F). Others may be quite correct in saying of you that you are interpreting x as F for yourself even when, as a result of believing that it is obvious to you that x is F, you believe that you know that x is F. For from the fact that you believe that you know x to be F, or find it obvious that x is F, it does not follow that you know x to be F, or that it is obvious to you that x is F.

It may also be natural for others to describe you as interpreting if they are unaware that it is obvious to you that x is F, that you know x to be F. If, for example, x's being F were not obvious to them because they were wedded to certain false beliefs, or did not have the requisite knowledge or skills, they might suppose that it only seemed obvious to you that x was F. But here, I believe, if it is obvious to you that x is F – you do in fact know it, and know that you know – then they would be mistaken if they said, concerning you, that you were interpreting. If I am right about this, a restricted version of (I) could be correct.

What frequently happens in critical interpretation in the arts is that people do not know whether the claims a critic makes are true or not, and hence they assume that the critic's claim that something is obvious to him, however categorically it is stated, should be regarded as a claim that something seems obvious to him. If the claim is so regarded, it is not odd to describe the critic as interpreting. However, if the critic's claim comes later to be regarded as literally correct, then what was earlier thought to be an interpretation may be reclassified as a description.

Although it is true that what is seen as obvious at one time need not be seen as obvious at another, and that in light of this we frequently take the 'obvious' remarks of earlier generations of critics to be interpretations – 'Most of the allegorical interpreters of Homer or of the Bible . . . would claim that their interpretations are in fact descriptions of Homer or of the Bible . . . However, given our different standards of textual criticism, what they claimed to be descriptions, we would admit only as interpretations.'[16] – in these cases we are not dealing with something that is obvious but only with something that seemed obvious. These cases would not show that the restricted version of (I) was incorrect, but rather that (Is) was incorrect:

> (Is) If it seems obvious to a person that x is F, then that person is not interpreting x as F.

If (Ir) is correct, although neither (I) or (Is) is, then not being obvious to one is a necessary condition for interpreting for oneself, or alternatively, being obvious to one is a sufficient condition for not interpreting for oneself. Not being obvious to one is not, however, a sufficient condition for interpreting for oneself, nor, therefore, is being obvious to one a necessary condition for not interpreting for oneself. When an intelligence officer attempts to break a code, although the solution is not obvious to him, his activity is not described as interpreting.

Is there then the following significant link between interpreting and the obvious: not being obvious to one is a necessary condition for interpreting for oneself (or, being obvious to one is a sufficient condition for not interpreting for oneself)? The objections to this link that I have so far considered have been, I claimed, the result of not bearing in mind the distinction between 'is obvious' and 'seems obvious'. I want to consider another objction, however, which does not seem to depend upon this.

I think it is clear that, in certain contexts, we often describe others as interpreting for themselves when we know that it is obvious to them that x is F. If we are correct in doing this in the contexts in question, then it seems that not being obvious to one cannot, after all, be a necessary condition for interpreting for oneself.

For example, in discussions of perception it is frequently said that all perceptual experience 'involves genuine interpretation, or judgement'.[17] In some of its uses, 'interpreting' is roughly equivalent to 'taking a given thing in some way', 'taking x to be F', and if we think of taking a thing in some way as classifying,

'classifying x as F'. In this use – let us call it 'interpreting*' – not being obvious to one is not a necessary condition for interpreting* for oneself. For example, one would be interpreting* for oneself if one labelled the object before one a tree, and it was obvious to one that the object was a tree. This, however, is not the sort of 'interpreting' that we are after, for all classifying is interpreting*. The relevant distinction between kinds of classifying, e.g., between calling a novel long and calling it enigmatic, could not be made in terms of interpreting*.

There is another sort of 'interpreting' where not being obvious to one is also not a necessary condition for interpreting for oneself. In some discussions about perception, 'interpreting' is not equivalent to 'taking a given thing in some way', but to 'taking a given thing in some way rather than another', taking x to be F rather than G', where F and G may be equally plausible ways of taking x, or where each way of taking x is at least plausible from a not unreasonable point of view. Let us call this 'interpreting**'.

If one takes x to be F rather than G, one is taking x to be F, although the reverse is not the case (there may be only one way of taking x). Interpreting of this sort, interpreting**, involves classifying, but only some classifying need be interpreting**, viz., that classifying in which it is assumed that more than a single way of taking is possible.[18] If it is possible for A to take x to be F rather than G when it is obvious to A that x is F, then not being obvious to one is not a necessary condition for interpreting** for oneself.

Although some philosophers may have meant interpreting** when they have spoken about critical interpreting in the arts, I believe there is a third sort of interpreting for oneself where not only does one take x to be F, or take x to be F rather than G, but also it is the case that it is not obvious to one that x is F, or that x is F rather than G. It is this sort of interpreting that I have been discussing; I shall continue to refer to it as interpreting. The following example illustrates these different sorts.

A poem appearing in an ink-wash sketch by Kung Hsien, a seventeenth century Chinese painter, reads: 'On the mountainside thorny brambles mix with fragrant orchids; the orchids, with their pervasive fragrance, hide the bramble clusters. The brambles, as firewood, will be picked by the woodcutters, leaving behind the orchids to survive the cold winter.' An art historian, commenting upon this work, identifies the brambles as 'collaborators with the Manchus', and the orchids with 'Chinese gentlemen such as Kung himself'.[19] Suppose it were true that in this work the brambles are to be identified as collaborators, and the expert in Chinese art who knows this finds it obvious. If this is obvious to him, then he is not, in the third sort of 'interpreting' I have specified above, interpreting for himself that the brambles are collaborators in Kung's poem, although he is interpreting*, viz., he is taking the brambles for collaborators, and in all probability he is interpreting**, taking the brambles for collaborators rather than . . . . He can also be interpreting for others that this is the case.

The concept of interpreting for oneself, with not being obvious to one as a necessary condition, is, I would contend, a useful one for discussing critical interpretation in the arts. It helps to explain why we speak of only some critical activity as interpreting. For example, consider Hans Baldung's picture *The Groom Bewitched*. In it we see a groom lying on the floor. Art critics have wondered whether the groom was dead, possessed by evil spirits or merely drunk. Given one usual way of identifying sets of predicates, alternative sets are available – 'dead'/'alive', 'possessed'/'not possessed', 'drunk'/'sober'. It has not been obvious to critics which set is the appropriate one. We speak of these critics as interpreting. If, instead of regarding these sets as alternatives, we regarded 'drunk'/'dead'/'possessed' as a single set, then the critical uncertainty would not be about which set but about which predicate from within the set applied. In either case it is not obvious to one what predicate applies.

It has in contrast been obvious to anyone with the ability to read pictures that the figure on the floor is a man (and if they know about grooms, a groom), that the man (groom) is lying on the floor. We do not ordinarily speak of the critic who says 'the figure on the floor is a man', or 'the man is lying on the floor', as interpreting the figure on the floor as a man or the man as lying on the floor. He knows that the figure on the floor is a man, that the man is lying on the floor, and he knows this without any special effort on his part.

Interpreting and the known

Although I believe this concept of interpreting for oneself to be useful for discussing critical activity in the arts, its usefulness depends upon the relationship between the obvious and knowing which we discussed earlier. Whereas being obvious to one is a sufficient condition for not interpreting for oneself, not being obvious to one is only a necessary condition for interpreting for oneself. Moreover, although not being obvious to one is a necessary condition for this form of interpreting, it turns out that this condition is itself entailed by another condition, a condition which is also necessary.

Suppose, for example, I know that your friend is preoccupied with his family problems, not irritated with you. Although I know this, it does not follow that it is obvious to me that your friend is preoccupied. Not all that we know is also obvious to us. Yet in this case I am not interpreting for myself that he is preoccupied since I know that I know that he is, and hence there is no epistemic possibility that I can be mistaken about it. A consideration of the earlier argument in support of (4r) indicates that in addition to it not being obvious to one that x is F, interpreting for oneself requires also that it be the case that one does not knowingly know that x is F. ('One knowingly knows that . . .' corresponds in sense to 'one knows that . . . and one knows that one knows that . . .') But if one's not knowingly knowing that x is F is taken to be a necessary requirement for interpreting for oneself,[20] and one's not knowingly knowing that x is F entails that it is not obvious to one that x is F, then is its not being obvious to one that x is F needed as a separate requirement? That is, obviousness does not seem to throw any light on (non-) interpretation that is not thrown on it by knowingly knowing. We seem to have gotten the full explanation when we get to knowingly knowing; the explanatory force of obviousness is merely parasitic or derivative.

The suggestion is that if it were the case that:

(1) A's knowingly knowing that x is F is sufficient for A's not interpreting x as F for himself, and

(2) it is obvious to A that x is F is sufficient for A's knowingly knowing that x is F,

then, although it is obvious to A that x is F is also sufficient for A's not interpreting x as F for himself, it looks as if it is not needed as a separate requirement for it. Given (2), A's knowingly knowing that x is F would suffice. However, this is the case only if the following condition is met:

There is no s, such that:

   (i) it is obvious to A that x is F is sufficient for s.
   (ii) s is sufficient for A's not interpreting x as F for himself.
   (iii) s is not sufficient for A's knowingly knowing that x is F.

That is, as (i), (ii), (iii) illustrate, it is logically possible given (1) and (2) for there to be something (viz., s) about the obvious in addition to its being knowing knowledge that also enables it to exclude interpreting. For example, suppose 's' were 'that x is F is a conclusion A has already got to'. That it is obvious to A that x is F is sufficient for 'x is F' being a conclusion A has already got to. If, moreover, 'x is F' being a conclusion A has already got to were sufficient for A's not interpreting x as F for himself, then, since one can reach a conclusion one does not know to be true (it might, for example, be a false conclusion), it would follow that something about the obvious other than its being knowing knowledge excluded interpreting.

' "x is F" is a conclusion A has already got to' is not, however, a satisfactory candidate for 's'. Since it is possible for a person to come (again) to a conclusion he has already got to, 'x is F' being a conclusion A has already got to is not sufficient for A's not interpreting x as F for himself. For example, A may believe a work to be enigmatic as a result of believing that certain features of the work are puzzling. Re-examining the work at some later time, A comes to believe that other features are puzzling, and concludes once again that the work is enigmatic. If on the occasion of re-examining the work A comes to believe, but not to know, the work to be enigmatic, then A can, on that occasion, be interpreting the work as enigmatic despite the fact that A has already, on the earlier occasion, got to the conclusion that it is.

That one candidate for *s* is unsatisfactory does not, of course, show that other candidates will also be unsatisfactory. However, I know of no satisfactory candidate for *s*. I shall, therefore, assume that its being knowledge and not its being something else is what makes its being obvious to A that *x* is *F* exclude A's interpreting *x* as *F* for himself.

While one wants to say that statements about the obvious in a work of art should not be counted as interpretations, one does not want to say that a critic who believes that some feature of a work is obvious is never thereby interpreting the work as having that feature. In this chapter I showed why these two wants are not incompatible. While what is obvious to a critic cannot yield an interpretation *for that critic*, it nevertheless can yield an interpretation *for others*.

What is obvious to a critic prevents the critic from interpreting for himself because what is obvious to him is what he knowingly knows. His knowingly knowing eliminates the possibility of his making a certain kind of mistake, yet without this possibility of mistake he cannot be interpreting for himself. In the next chapter I examine in more detail the links so far established between interpreting, the obvious, and the known.

Notes

1 Ludwig Wittgenstein, *Philosophical Investigations* (New York, 1969), p. 212e.
2 Unless context dictates otherwise, the various forms of this pronoun should be understood hereafter in the gender neutral sense.
3 William Kennick, *Art and Philosophy* (2nd edn), p. 372. When Kennick speaks of anyone in 'anyone can see this at a glance', he does not, of course, mean literally anyone – newborn infants, mental defectives, madmen, are, for starters, to be excluded. Rather he means anyone who has certain minimal abilities and capacities.
4 I am not claiming that it is a decidable issue whether the character is avoiding love. If it were a decidable issue, however, and it could be shown that the character was not avoiding love, then it could not have been obvious that he was avoiding love. If the issue is not a decidable one, then the critic's claim that it is obvious to him that the character is avoiding love may nevertheless be defeated. Cf. chapter 7, pp. 113–14.

5 Wittgenstein, *Philosophical Investigations*, p. 212e.
6 If one falsely believes that one knows that x is F, then as far as one knows, it is still possible for one to be mistaken about x being F. Suppose I falsely believe that I know that someone at my dinner has a Picasso, because although someone at my dinner has one, I don't know this. Here it would be epistemically possible for me to be mistaken about x being F, although it would not be metaphysically possible for me to be mistaken.
7 Kennick, *Art and Philosophy* (2nd edn), p. 373.
8 Robert Matthews, 'Describing and interpreting a work of art', *Journal of Aesthetics and Art Criticism* vol. XXXVI (Fall 1977), 5–14.
9 Cf., for example, n. 20 below and chapter 8, p. 145.
10 Matthews, 'Describing and interpreting a work of art', 8.
11 Ibid., 7.
12 Michael Hancher, 'Afterwords', *Journal of Aesthetics and Art Criticism* vol. XXXVI (Summer 1978); both quotations appear on 484.
13 Ibid.
14 Wittgenstein, *Philosophical Investigations*, p. 193e.
15 Hancher, 'Afterwords', 484.
16 Laurent Stern, 'On interpreting', *Journal of Aesthetics and Art Criticism* vol. XXXIX (Winter 1980), 128 n. 12.
17 Roger Scruton, *Art and Imagination*, p. 115.
18 If, as some philosophers have argued, a multiplicity of equally plausible ways of taking what is perceived exist, either on the phenomenal or the physical level, then all classifying in the perceptual realm, all taking x to be F, would also always be taking x to be F rather than G. Hence, on this account, all classifying in this realm would involve interpreting**. If it were the case that in the arts, in any classifying that one does, alternative classifications were also always available, then here too all classifying would be interpreting**. If it were, one could not, using 'interpret**', distinguish between kinds of classifying.

Whether in any classifying in art criticism there are always the right kind of alternatives available, viz., ones that are at least plausible from a not unreasonable point of view, is a complicated issue. Consider a novel which extends over more than 700 standard pages. The work is generally regarded as long, indeed it seems obvious to people that it is long. But the novel is long because certain things are assumed to be the case. It is long given a certain comparison class – *Ulysses* is long when compared with *The Possessed* or *Gulliver's Travels*. Given another comparison class, viz., *Remembrance of Things Past*, or *War and Peace*, *Ulysses* might not be long. There is nothing, moreover, in the work itself to make only one comparison class a viable one. Here, however, one might claim that once a given comparison class is set, 'long' is the only plausible candidate. But this is not true. It is only after one has restricted the set of predicates, for example, to 'long' and 'short', that 'long' might be the only plausible candidate. Given that different degrees of precision are possible, for some purposes it might be reasonable to introduce other predicates – 'between long and short', 'between long and between-long-and-short', and so on.

In order to decide whether any predicate applies to a given thing we must settle at least two questions – what the realm of discourse is, and what the set of alternatives within that realm is. If, in certain circumstances, the realm and the set of alternatives within that realm are habitually fixed, then we may not want to say, of the person who says that *x* is *F*, that he is interpreting**, although he would be interpreting*. For a further discussion of some of these issues, see chapter 5, pp. 71–2.

19 *New Yorker* (13 July 1981), 24, 23.
20 This requirement of not knowingly knowing that *x* is *F* is, unlike Matthews's requirement of not being in a position to know, limited to a specific form of interpreting, interpreting for oneself, and to a specific sense of 'interpreting' for oneself. Moreover, a critic may be in a position to know whether *x* is *F*, but not know it, and hence may be interpreting *x* as *F*. For example, a critic may, if I understand Matthews's notion of being in a position to know, be in such a position with regard to whether a character has *n* numbers of daughters, but not know that he does since he has made a mistake in reading one of the character's remarks.

This requirement of not knowingly knowing would not make it impossible for an interpretation to be correct, for on the account I have given, one can knowingly know that *x* is *F* and yet interpret *x* as *F* for others. If the statement one gives to another when one interprets for him is considered to be an interpretation, then presumably it could be correct. It is also possible that when one interprets for oneself, although one does not know that one's interpretation is correct, it could turn out that it was.

3

Interpreting, the Obvious
and the Known
Part II

If what I have said in chapter 2 is correct, then the following four claims are true:

(I)   If it is obvious to A that x is F, then A is not interpreting x as F for himself.

(II) If A knowingly knows that x is F, then A is not interpreting x as F for himself.

(III) Its being obvious to A that x is F prevents A from interpreting x as F for himself because
  (1) that it is obvious to A that x is F entails that A knowingly knows that x is F, and
  (2) (=(II)) If A knowingly knows that x is F, then A is not interpreting x as F for himself.

(IV) That A knowingly knows that x is F prevents A from interpreting x as F for himself because
  (1) if A knowingly knows that x is F, then it is not epistemically possible for A to be mistaken about x being F, it is not possible for it to prove false that x is F, and
  (2) unless it is epistemically possible for A to be mistaken about x being F, A cannot interpret x as F for himself.

For simplicity let us use some abbreviations: 'O' for 'it is obvious to A that x is F', 'K' for 'A knowingly knows that x is F', 'I' for 'A interprets x as F for himself', and 'NM' for 'it is not epistemically possible for A to be mistaken about x being F'. (I) through (IV) become:

(I)   O prevents I
(II)   K prevents I
(III) O prevents I because (1) O entails K and (2) K prevents I
(IV) K prevents I because (1) K entails NM and (2) NM prevents I

In the previous chapter I answered some objections to these claims; in this chapter I shall answer others.

A   For some verbs, when one has (just) —ed, in many cases, one —s. For example, if you have just concluded that Orwell's *Animal Farm* is about totalitarianism, then, normally, you conclude that *Animal Farm* is about totalitarianism. If 'interpret' is like 'conclude' in this regard, then when A has interpreted *Animal Farm* as about totalitarianism, it may also be the case that A interprets *Animal Farm* as about totalitarianism. But suppose that in such a case, after having interpreted *Animal Farm* as about totalitarianism, A comes to know that *Animal Farm* is about totalitarianism; then in what might be called the 'result' sense of 'interpret', (viz., one continues to hold an interpretation already formed) A interprets *Animal Farm* as about totalitarianism for himself, even though A knows that *Animal Farm* is about totalitarianism. In this sense of 'interpret', claim (II) (K prevents I) would be false (as would (III) and (IV)).

However, it is what might be called the 'process' sense of 'interpret', (viz., one forms an interpretation) and not the 'result' sense that I am interested in. The claim in (II) is to be understood as:

> If A knowingly knows that x is F, then A is not now interpreting x as F for himself.

In what follows "interpret" bears its process sense.

B   One can imagine situations in which knowingly knowing that something is the case is not accompanied by understanding what its being the case involves. Suppose, for example, that some critics knowingly knew that *The Turn of the Screw* was a story about stories (I shall for simplicity use 'know$_k$' for 'knowingly knows'.) Suppose, moreover, that certain other critics knew$_k$ this indirectly by knowing that the first critics knew this. (These suppositions are not uncontroversial.) If one of the second critics had adequate warrant for such a knowledge claim, he might still not understand what the story's being about stories involved, not know why it was as it was. Would this critic not have room to interpret it as this kind of story for himself despite the fact that he knows$_k$ that it is?

C Or suppose, for example, that a person knew$_k$, without learning so from someone else, that *The Turn of the Screw* was a story about stories, but had forgotten what its being one involved, why it was one. If, in trying to regain his prior understanding, he had room to interpret it as a story about stories for himself, then (II) (K prevents I) would be false (as would (III) and (IV)).

D Or imagine that a person who knows$_k$ that *The Turn of the Screw* is a story about stories, and why it is a story about stories, is able by one means or another, e.g., by re-reading the work, or by reading another critic, or . . . , to deepen his understanding of it. Would he, when doing this, be interpreting *The Turn of the Screw* as a story about stories for himself despite his knowing that it is?

E Some of the things we know$_k$ others may dispute. If one re-examines one's grounds for a knowledge claim, not to remind oneself of its truth, but in response to a critical attack, and if in this re-examining process, one could be interpreting for oneself, then (II), (III), and (IV) would be false.

Although I acknowledged that in some sorts of 'interpreting' not knowing$_k$ x to be F is not a necessary condition of interpreting for oneself (that is, if we regard 'interpret x as F' as roughly 'take x to be F' or 'take x to be F rather than G'), I claimed that it is a necessary condition of one sort of 'interpreting' useful for art criticism. Examples B, C, D, and E are attempts to show that no such sort of interpreting exists: A's not knowing$_k$ x to be F is for no sort of 'interpreting' a necessary condition of A's interpreting x as F for himself.

In objections B through E, it is claimed that (II) (K prevents I) is incorrect, and if it were one could show that (IV (2)) (NM prevents I) was incorrect ((IV) as a whole as well as (III) would also be incorrect). The argument in these objections is a simple one. Since it is possible that when A knows$_k$ x to be F, A nevertheless interprets x as F for himself, it follows that A's not knowing$_k$ x to be F is not a necessary condition of A's interpreting x as F for himself. Objections B through E purport to give cases in which A knows$_k$ that x is F, yet A is interpreting x as F for himself. Moreover, if A's knowing$_k$ x to be F entails its being epistemically impossible for A to be mistaken about x being F (it is not possible for it to prove false that x is F), then, were any of these objections B through E well taken, it would follow that its being epistemically possible for A to be mistaken about x being F is not a necessary condition of A's interpreting x as F for himself.

We can consider objections B, C, and D together. The first thing to notice about these objections is that whether they are correct or not depends upon the standard of acceptability appropriate for interpretations. That is, if interpretations did not take the values 'true' and 'false', these three objections could not arise. For example, suppose that those critical classifications of artworks which count as interpretations could never be known, since they could not be true, they are not the sorts of things that take the value 'true' (assuming here that knowledge requires at least justified true belief); then claim (II) – if A knowingly knows that x is F, then A is not interpreting x as F for himself – would have to be correct, if x were an artwork. For, on this supposition, if A knew$_k$ that *The Turn of the Screw* was a story about stories, then A would not be interpreting it as a story about stories for himself (an interpretation can't be true and hence the statements constituting it can't be known to be true); if A were interpreting it as a story about stories for himself, then A would not know that it was such. Objections, B, C, and D, therefore, rely on critical classifications being true and false, and if truth and falsity are applied only to statements, on these classifications being statements.

Objections B through D pose a serious, but not, I think, insurmountable, problem for those who hold that interpretations are statements for which the values 'true' and 'false' are not inappropriate. Since there are many who hold this view, I shall try to meet these objections.

A distinction is made in these three objections between knowing that something is the case and understanding what its being the case involves or understanding why it is as it is. If (as seems reasonable to suppose) it is possible to know$_k$ that x is F in the sense of *knowing$_k$ is to be the case that x is F without understanding why x is F*, then (these objections suggest) one could interpret *x* as *F* for oneself, one could come to understand why *x* is *F*, even though one knew$_k$ that *x* is *F* was the case. These objections suggest that it is not a lack of relevant knowledge that is required for interpreting for oneself, but a lack of relevant understanding. Substituting 'understands why' for 'knowingly knows' in (II), would not entirely meet these objections, for in objection D it is assumed that when A understands why *x* is *F*, A can yet interpret *x* as *F* for himself. In objection D one is only deepening one's understanding.

One way of meeting these objections would be to (1) replace 'know that *x* is *F*' with 'fully know that *x* is *F*' and (2) require A fully to know that *x* is *F*. That is:

> (II) If A knowingly fully knows that *x* is *F* (A knowingly knows that *x* is *F* and knowingly fully understands why *x* is *F* and what *x*'s being *F* involves), then A is not interpreting *x* as *F* for himself.

Partial or incomplete knowledge doesn't block interpreting for oneself, full knowledge does. Allowing 'knowledge' to refer to more than a species of justified true belief is, for example, recommended by Nelson Goodman:

> Much of knowing aims at something other than true, or any, belief. An increase in acuity of insight or in range of comprehension, rather than a change in belief, occurs when we find in a pictured forest a face we already knew was there, or learn to distinguish stylistic differences among works already classified by artist or composer or writer, or study a picture or a concerto or a treatise until we see or hear or grasp features and structures we could not discern before. Such growth in knowledge is not by formation or fixation of belief but by the advancement of understanding.[1]

If it is difficult or impossible in some situations fully to understand why *x* is *F*, what *x*'s being *F* involves (e.g., what Willy Loman's deception in Arthur Miller's *Death of a Salesman* involves or what being a story about stories involves), then on the new reading of (II) there could be room in these situations to interpret *x* as *F* for oneself. However, one needs to be careful about what one would be doing in these situations. If A knows$_k$ that Willy Loman is deceiving himself, then no one takes A's interpreting Willy as deceiving himself standardly to involve Willy deceiving himself *simpliciter*. A interprets Willy as deceiving himself in the sense that A deepens his understanding of what such deception involves. Nevertheless, although it is true that not all deepening of one's understanding is interpreting for oneself – for example, when deepening his understanding of how an automobile engine works, A is not thereby interpreting the engine for himself – some cases of increasing one's understanding do seem to involve interpreting for oneself.

I have so far assumed that one could know that x is F without also understanding why x is F. However, circumstances frequently require that, when one knows that x is F, one also understands why x is F and what x's being F involves. For example, if one were required to acquire one's knowledge about certain properties of artworks first hand (either because of the unavailability or impossibility or undesirability of any other authority), then in order for one to know that x is F, one must be able to give reasons for x's being F. But in order to give the appropriate sort of reasons here, one needs to understand why x is F and what x's being F involves. For example, a person who knows that a piece of music, e.g., the minuet of Mozart's string quartet in A, is unified, needs to understand what its being unified involved and why it was unified. If he did not understand these things, then he would not be able to give the right sort of reasons (assuming he acquires his knowledge first hand).

Another way of handling objections B through D would be to distinguish between the object known and the object interpreted. If any of these three objections were correct, then A could interpret x as F, for example, Willy as a self deceiver, when A knew$_k$ that x is F, Willy is a self-deceiver. Suppose, however, that when A knows$_k$ that x is F, that Willy is a self-deceiver, 'x' is 'Willy' and 'F' is 'a self-deceiver', but when A interprets x as F, the 'x' is not 'Willy' but 'Willy-as-self-deceiver' and the 'F' is not 'a self-deceiver' but '——', the '——' being filled in by whatever A's understanding of the self-deceiving involves. If, as suggested here, the 'x's' and the 'F's' are distinct in the two activities, then in the cases described in B through D, one would not both know that x is F and interpret x as F for oneself for the same values of 'x' and 'F'. This way of handling the objections has the advantage of leaving the original (II) unchanged, for it is not required that 'fully' be put before 'knows' or that 'know' include 'understand'.

In E it was claimed that when one re-examines one's ground for a knowledge claim, not to remind oneself of its truth, but in response to a critical attack, one could be interpreting for oneself. Claim (II) (K prevents I) would seem to be false. However, if in such a re-examining process A comes to a deeper understanding of why x is F, then A can be interpreting x as F for himself, without it being the case that (II) (K prevents I) is false. A's interpreting x as F for himself in this case would be explainable on either of the above hypotheses – either A had not fully known$_k$ that x is F before, or what A discovers in the re-examining process is not the same 'x' and 'F' he asserted he knew. If A simply rehearsed for the other what his grounds were, then A would be interpreting x as F for this other but not for himself.

Suppose one can handle objections A through E in the ways I have suggested. Either of the two ways of handling objections B through E does so equally well. There are, nevertheless, further objections to my four claims.

F One might want to challenge the explanation I give in (IV) (K prevents I because (1) K entails NM and (2) NM prevents I) of why, when A knows$_k$ that x is F, this excludes A from interpreting x as F for himself, even if one did not want to question the truth of (II) (K prevents I) or (I) (O prevents I). It might be alleged, for example, that when it is not epistemically possible for A to be mistaken about x being F (i.e., it is not possible for it to prove false that x is F) this is sometimes the case not due to A's knowing$_k$ that x is F, but due to x's being F not being the kind of thing that A could know or be mistaken about – that x is F is neither true nor false and hence it is not possible for it to prove false that x is F. If in such a situation A could nevertheless interpret x as F for himself, then condition (IV(2)) (NM prevents I) would be incorrect, even if (II) (K prevents I) were correct.

Whereas we saw that in objections B through E, it was claimed that (II) (K prevents I) was incorrect (and if it were, then one could show that (IV(2)) (NM prevents I) was incorrect), the present allegation is that condition (IV(2)) is incorrect whether or not (II) is correct. The argument here is this: when it is neither true nor false that x is F, it is not epistemically possible for A to be mistaken about x being F, it is not possible for it to prove false that x is F. Since it is nevertheless possible in these situations that A interprets x as F for himself (the argument continues), it follows that its being epistemically possible for A to be mistaken about x being F cannot be a necessary condition for A's interpreting x as F for himself. For example, although philosophers of law argue about whether certain appellate decisions are neither true nor false, they believe that the judges making such decisions are interpreting for themselves. If we decided that these judicial decisions were neither true nor false, then its being epistemically possible for A to be mistaken about x being F, its being possible for it to prove false that x is F, would not be a necessary condition of A's interpreting x as F for himself.

It is worth noticing here that one could jointly maintain objections B through E and F only under certain conditions. That is, so long as the classifications that a defender of F holds to be neither true nor false are classifications other than those held by a defender of B through E to be known, and thus true, there would be no difficulty in defending these objections jointly.

If, however, a defender of F believed that some or all of those classifications which B through E claimed were known, and hence true, were neither true nor false, and thus not known, then F, rather than being compatible with all or some of these objections would show why some or all of these objections must fail. For, as we saw earlier, in order for B through E to show (II) (K prevents I) incorrect, it must be the case that A knows$_k$ x to be F. If, as F maintains, that x is F were not the kind of thing that is either true or false, then A could not know$_k$ that x is F.

There are defenders of F^2 who would claim that some of the classifications about which I have raised the possibility that they might be known – for example, that *The Turn of the Screw* is a story about stories, that a character is deceived or is avoiding love – are classifications which are neither true nor false and hence not known. That is, if we limit 'x is F' to critical classifications, we find disagreement about whether some classifications are neither true nor false, and this disagreement includes those classifications which have been called interpretations. In order, therefore, not to beg the question at this stage of the discussion about which epithets of value are appropriate to which classifications, I must handle objection F.

I shall do this by emending the notion of mistake in (IV(2)). That is, the notion of the epistemic possibility of a mistake would no longer be linked exclusively with the notion of the possibility of a hypothesis proving false. While the defenders of F would claim that interpretive classifications cannot be true, they would acknowledge that these classifications can be plausible or reasonable or defensible or supportable. Given this, claim (IV(2)) emended would be:

> IV(2)E) Unless it is epistemically possible for A to be mistaken about x being F – *that is*, unless it is possible for it to prove false that, or implausible that, or unsupportable that, or unreasonable that, or indefensible that x is F – A cannot interpret x as F for himself.

(IV(1)) would need a similar reformulation:

> (IV(1)E) If A knowingly knows that x is F, then it is not epistemically possible for A to be mistaken about x being F, it is not possible for it to prove false that, or implausible that, or unsupportable that, or unreasonable that, or indefensible that x is F.

The general point I wish to make in (IV(2)) (NM prevents I) is not dependent upon adopting some one standard of acceptability for the classification 'x is F'. That is, whether the classification is true or false, neither true nor false, false but not true, and so on, does not affect whether it must be epistemically possible for A to be mistaken about x being F, if A is interpreting x as F. If, for example, certain critical classifications were neither true nor false, but took the values 'plausible', or certain judicial decisions were more or less reasonable but not true or false, then it would still be the case that in order for A to interpret x as F for himself, it must be epistemically possible for A to be mistaken about x being F.

If it were epistemically impossible for A to be mistaken, understanding this according to the emended version of (IV(2)), then A would not be interpreting for himself. What A would be doing would depend on the particular circumstances. Matthews, for example, claims that in order to interpret one must believe that one has some evidence which supports one's classification. Interpretations are not conjectures or guesses, for whereas the latter do not require that one be able to 'justify' them, interpretations do. We must, he says, be in a position to know whether the statements constituting the interpretations 'are plausible, reasonable, or at least defensible on evidence provided by the interpretandum'.[3] Arnold Isenberg has noted that '[e]ven if there were no truth or falsity in criticism, there would still be agreement and disagreement; and there would be argument which arises out of disagreement and attempts to resolve it.'[4] Suppose, for example, that a judge proclaims that a contract is valid, without being able to give any reasons why it is. We would not regard him as interpreting. Nor would a critic who said that a character was avoiding love be interpreting the character as avoiding love if he had not considered what the character did. He would only be doing something along the lines of guessing or conjecturing that the character was avoiding love.

I have argued that (I), (II), (III) and (IV), with minor emendation, can be defended when one leaves open the question of what epithets of value apply to the classifications. Can the question – what status do the classifications have? – be similarly left open? For example, if 'x is F' were not a statement about the work but a report of a kind of experience, would claims (I) through (IV) be true?

G Suppose interpreting x as F involved, for a large class of objects, including art objects, seeing x as F or hearing x as F, and seeing or hearing-as was a peculiar kind of experience – what might be called 'thought-impregnated' experience. For example, Roger Scruton sugests ' "[s]eeing as" is like an "unasserted" visual experience: it is the embodiment of a thought which, if "asserted", would amount to a genuine perception'.[5] The suggestion is that in interpreting one is reporting that one has had a certain kind of experience, one has experienced x as F. One is not stating that x is F, that x has the property F.

Imagine that A knows$_k$ that a sequence of notes is a melody and it is not epistemically possible for A to be mistaken about whether the sequence is a melody. Imagine too that A has not yet heard the sequence as a melody. That one could know$_k$ without having the requisite experience is suggested in the following:

> it is impossible not to be fully aware of the powerful base line, with its emphatic octaves counteracting the melting treble part. But how many listeners are able to hear the melody of the treble repeated in these muttering octaves? It may require considerable effort to hear these notes as a melody even though, from the very nature of the case, one knows already what the melody is.[6]

Now imagine that A comes to have the requisite experience. If A, in having this experience, could be said to interpret the sequence as a melody, then (II) (III(2)) (K prevents I) and (IV(2)) (NM) prevents I) would be false.

Whether this kind of case poses a genuine threat to claims (II) and (IV(2)), as emended, depends upon the nature of the relationship between interpreting and experiencing-as. If experiencing-as were only necessary, but not sufficient, for interpreting, then the imagined case would not affect these claims.

The emended version of (II) at which we arrived in discussing objections B through E – A is required knowingly fully to know that x is F, for interpreting to be ruled out – need not conflict with the view that interpreting x as F, for a large range of x's, *essentially involves* a special kind of experience. There need be no conflict even if we suppose that full understanding includes experiencing-as.

(IV(2)) – if it is not epistemically possible for A to be mistaken about x being F, then A is not interpreting x as F – also need not conflict with the view that interpreting x as F, for a large range of x's, *essentially* involves a special kind of experience. Imagine that A knows$_k$ that the sequence is a melody and it is not epistemically possible for A to be mistaken about the sequence being a melody. Suppose further that A is now hearing the sequence as a melody. If hearing-as is necessary but not sufficient for interpreting, then one need not suppose that A is in this situation interpreting x as F for himself.

Experiencing-as cannot, however, be both necessary and sufficient for interpreting. It cannot, that is, if we accept as essential to critical interpretation the 'phenomenon of a double-aspect'[7] – '[o]ne man can see a work of art as tragic, another as ironical (*Death in Venice*, say), both be able to justify their judgements to each other, and both refer to the same first-order features in doing so'.[8] Since the presence of this phenomenon in interpretation is integral to the view that interpreting involves experiencing-as, let us see why this is the case.

If interpreting requires experiencing-as, it is an experiencing-as which is done by an aurally or visually competent experiencer – on who has the background of behavior requisite for reasoned discrimination[9] – and which is justifiable in terms of the first-order features of the work. The double-aspect phenomenon arises when there is justificatory parity among the various experiencings-as; when it is not the case that only one experiencing-as is right. If experiencing-as *simpliciter* were sufficient for interpreting, then the person who hears the notes as a melody and the person who hears the notes as a random sequence would both be interpreting. But in this same example, the double-aspect phenomenon could not arise, for the two experiencings-as would not have justificatory parity. The person who hears the sequence as a melody, when he knows that it is one, would be able to justify his experiencing-as in a way in which the person who hears the sequence as a random succession would not. For while one experiences an aspect of the work in an experiencing-as, 'being a melody' is in this example not only an aspect of the work, it is also a first-order feature of the work (this follows from the person's knowing the sequence to be a melody). 'Being a random succession' is not, in this example, a first-order feature of the work, so the aspect 'being a melody' gets a justification that the aspect 'being a random succession' does not. One of the experiencings-as in this situation would be right.

If we require that the experiencing-as that is sufficient for interpreting be the experiencing-as which has justificatory parity with any of the work's other experiencing-as, thus allowing for the double-aspect phenomenon, then the person who experiences the sequence as a melody when he knows that it is one would not be interpreting.

If experiencing-as were sufficient for interpreting, then claims (II) and (IV(2)), as emended, would be jeopardized. For it seems plausible to say that if one knowingly fully knows that x is F, then one is experiencing, or has experienced, x as F. But if experiencing x as F were sufficient for interpreting x as F for oneself, then when one knowingly fully knows that x is F one must be interpreting x as F for oneself. Further, if when one experiences x as F one is interpreting x as F, then the relevant sort of mistake required by (IV(2)) is not possible.

It seems arguable, however, that experiencing-as is not sufficient for interpreting for oneself; in particular, that cases of experiencing x as F when one knows$_k$ that x is F and one understands, short of experiencing x as F, why x is F and what x's being F involves are not cases of interpreting for oneself. Accordingly, any cases of interpreting x as F for oneself that involve experiencing x as F are cases in which one does not know$_k$ that x is F or one does not understand why x is F or what x's being F involves. In such cases it is epistemically possible to make the requisite sort of mistake.

While I have already mentioned one argument against sufficiency, since this argument relies on various assumptions which may be problematic – e.g., assumptions about the necessity of experiencing-as for interpreting and about the double-aspect phenomenon – this argument will not serve my purpose here. I shall instead appeal to an idea that can be expressed along more or less the following lines.

Consider two cases which involve experiencing-as. In the first case one tries to hear a sequence of notes as a melody when one knows$_k$ that the sequence is a melody and, except for hearing it as a melody, one understands why it is a melody and what its being a melody involves. In the second case one tries to determine, when one does not yet know, what the sequence can be heard-as. In the first case, while one can fail to hear the sequence as a melody, one cannot be mistaken as to its being one. In the second case one can, as far as one knows, be mistaken about what it can be heard-as, even if one believes, but does not know, that it is supposed to be heard as a melody. I want to exclude the relevant sort of interpreting for oneself from the first case. Moreover, I believe that this is not an arbitrary or *ad hoc* exclusion, since I believe that in the first case *there is nothing*, as it were, *to interpret* for oneself. One already knows$_k$ the sequence to be a melody, and one understands, short of hearing it as a melody, why it is a melody and what its being a melody involves. All that is required in this case is to hear the sequence as a melody for oneself.

An increase in understanding which is accomplished by one's *merely* experiencing x as F is to be contrasted with an increase in understanding which is accomplished by learning why x is F or learning what x's being F involves. On my account, in the latter cases, but not in the former, A can be interpreting x as F for himself, for in these latter cases A does not yet know what x's being F involves or why x is F, and hence it is possible for A to be mistaken about them. Consider, for example, understanding why *The Turn of the Screw* is a story about stories or what its being a story about stories involves. If I am right about this, then experiencing-as is not sufficient for interpreting for oneself, and claims (II) and (IV(2)), as emended, stand.

H Suppose one claimed that the relevant sort of experiencing x as F was not only necessary for understanding that x is F and hence for knowing that x is F, but was sufficient as well; then (II) ((III(2))) (K prevents I) and (IV(2)) (NM prevents I) would be false. That is, suppose that '[t]o see the sadness in the music and to know that the music is sad are one and the same thing.'[10] Suppose also that hearing the music as sad is nothing other than seeing the sadness in it. On these assumptions, experiencing x as F (assuming the experiencer to have the requisite background of behavior) would be *sufficient* for knowing that x is F. Thus, insofar as interpreting x as F involves experiencing x as F, when one interprets x as F one must know that x is F.

The position under discussion shows why the knowing$_k$ referred to in claim (II) ((III(2))) should not be identified with the sort of experiencing-as which, though thought-impregnated, is independent of believing that. Given that identification, it might be arguable that claim (II) was false. To know that x is F, as I am using the term 'know', involves at least having a justified true belief that x is F; it may also involve understanding why x is F, which in turn may involve experiencing x as F. Moreover, as we saw in G, the relevant kind of experiencing-as is not to be identified with interpreting for oneself, even if when one interprets x as F for oneself, one must hear or see x as F. For example, the person who finally hears the sounds as a melody, although he knew$_k$ that they were one, need not be interpreting the sounds as a melody for himself.

Believing that x is F, as I understand it, cannot, moreover, be equated with believing that x is literally F, for there are cases where interpreting x as F, if it involves classifying x, cannot be understood as classifying x as F *simpliciter*. For example, a critic who says the music is sad does not believe it to be literally sad. He may believe it to be metaphorically sad. However, I am stipulating that if A knows$_k$ that a work is metaphorically or literally F, and understands why it is F and what its being F involves, even though this knowing$_k$ and understanding is not sufficient for experiencing the work as F, A is not thereby interpreting x as F for himself when A comes to experience x as F.

I Suppose 'x is F' were neither a statement nor the report of a special kind of experience, but a prescription. The person who said 'x is F' was not stating that x was F, or reporting that he had a certain experience of x as F, but was rather recommending that one should regard x as F. On this view it is not being claimed that one knows$_k$ that x is F. Since it is possible that one does not know this, one could given (II) ((III(2))), interpret x as F for oneself. Claim (II) would not in such cases be challenged. Nor would (IV(2)) since it would be possible to be mistaken about whether the work should be read or seen or heard in the manner recommended.

Charles Stevenson, for example, claims that '[h]aving roughly familiarized himself with all the ways in which a work of art *can* be experienced, a critic must proceed to make a selection from among them – a *decision* about how he is to observe the work in the course of his subsequent appreciation.'[11] Although the decision here depends upon factors that are not merely logical or cognitive, such a decision may, nevertheless, be mistaken. For example, if the decision were based on inadequate knowledge of the object – the critic was not familiar enough with the object – then the decision so based could be mistaken. Suppose a critic recommends that one regard a work as unified, having overlooked certain disparate elements in the work which are later pointed out to him. In light of the new information he may agree that his earlier decision to regard the work as unified was mistaken. Since the reasons for a decision are many, if one is mistaken about any of them, one's subsequent decision could be mistaken.

In this chapter I have discussed how the substantial claims of the previous chapter would be affected by particular views about the status of an interpretive remark and the kind of value assigned to it. Although I have argued that these claims could be defended whatever particular views about status and value one adopts, in the next chapter I want to discuss whether there are reasons for preferring one status or value to another.

Notes

1 Nelson Goodman, *Ways of Worldmaking* (Indianapolis, 1978), pp. 21–2.
2 Cf. chapters 4 through 6.
3 Robert Matthews, 'Describing and interpreting a work of art', 8.
4 Arnold Isenberg, 'Critical communication', *Art and Philosophy*, Kennick ed., (2nd edn), 667 (n. 2).
5 Roger Scruton, *Art and Imagination*, p. 120.
6 Ibid., p. 174–5. Scruton is discussing a passage from Brahms' *Variations on a theme by Richard Schumann*.
7 Ibid., p. 122.
8 Ibid., p. 125.
9 Ibid., p. 181. Here Scruton argues that 'there must be a recognized background of "musical behaviour" before we can meaningfully attribute musical experiences to a man . . . It will involve preferences, choices, intentional activity, a sense of what is right and wrong.'
10 Ibid., p. 54.
11 Charles Stevenson, 'Interpretation and evaluation in aesthetics', Kennick ed., *Art and Philosophy* (1st edn), 477.

4

Status and Acceptability Standard: Truth and Intention

What is the status of, and what is the standard of acceptability for, the linguistic expression of critical interpretations of artworks? Are they statements, hypotheses, reports of special kinds of experience, prescriptions? Are they true or false, or only plausible, defensible, interesting or the like? Must we suppose them all to have a single status or acceptability standard? That is, if some were statements taking the values 'true' and 'false', would it follow that all are statements taking these values?

That critics put forward interpretive remarks in indicative form is undeniable.[1] ('Unmotivated treachery, for the mere intent of injury, and self-violence are Poe's obsessive subjects.'[2] 'Consider for example North Italian quattrocento altar-pieces that depict a woman bearing a platter of severed breasts. Those we know to be representations of St Agnes.'[3] 'The animated, elegant *Fortuna* is intended as the musical symbol of the pagan goddess . . .'[4] 'Obviously the satyr with his wine jug represents what we call "the powers of darkness" . . .'[5]) While the surface grammatical form of these remarks suggests they are statements, the question of status is not settled by surface grammatical form, for such form is not an unambiguous guide to status. For example, although 'What's the difference?' has the form of a question, in some contexts it may be used not to ask for the difference, but to assert that the speaker doesn't care what the difference is.[6]

Critical practice seems, moreover, to support the view that interpretive remarks are not always statements – critics seem to make recommendations about how to view artworks, to report experiences-as, to offer their interpretations as plausible hypotheses rather than as true statements. In addition, a number of philosophers and critics have claimed that, regardless of grammatical form, there are arguments to show that interpretive remarks *cannot* be statements.

I approach the question of the status of interpretive remarks by considering whether – and, if so, how – interpretive remarks are defeasible. Outside criticism there are models for the defeasibility of different kinds of remark. For example, an alleged statement of fact can be falsified; a scientific hypothesis can be disconfirmed; a political prescription can be undermined by showing that it cannot be obeyed; the report of a gestalt seeing-as can be discredited by showing that the experiencer lacked some ability requisite to the having of such an experience. If interpretive remarks in art criticism had the same status as any of these other remarks, if they were, for example, statements, hypotheses, prescriptions, or reports of experiences-as, then they would be subject to the kinds of defeasibility appropriate to remarks of that status.

The suggestion here is that if an interpretive remark has a certain status, then it will be defeasible in certain ways. If we look to critical practice, as I propose we do, to see what it reveals about the presence of these kinds of defeasibility, we would not thereby have determined what status(es) critical interpretations had, unless, that is, kinds of defeasibility were sufficient for kinds of status. I shall argue that one important kind of defeasibility – defeat by a relevant counterpossibility – is sufficient in art criticism for one kind of status – that of statement. If this kind of defeat is, as I believe, typical in art criticism, then we shall have sufficient reason for regarding many critical interpretive remarks as statements. This kind of defeat, moreover, has the advantage of being compatible with multiple interpretations. I discuss other kinds of defeasibility that are not sufficient for status, for different statuses share some modes of defeat. Showing, however, that an interpretive remark is not defeasible in a given way can show that the remark does not have a certain status if being defeasible in this way is necessary for this status. My looking to critical practice to discover which, if any, of these kinds of defeasibility are appropriate to interpretive remarks can, therefore, take us varying distances toward determining what status these remarks have. In some cases, and these are important and typical cases, a unique status can be established, in other cases, certain statuses can be ruled out, in still others, it will be evident that the question of status can only be settled by appealing to further features of critical practice. The question of acceptability standard will be discussed in conjunction with the question of status.

This appeal to critical practice is a legitimate one, however, only if a certain objection can be dealt with. Some philosophers and critics have attempted to settle the question of status and acceptability standard, not by looking at critical practice, but by offering pre-emptive arguments to the effect that, given what meanings are, given what texts are, given what art works are . . . , certain candidate statuses and acceptability standards for interpretive remarks are a priori ruled out. If I am not to be guilty of begging the question of the status and acceptability standard of interpretive remarks by using, as I do, critical practice as the touchstone for testing theories of interpretation, then these arguments must be dealt with.

I divide these arguments into two kinds. The first kind argues directly against one particular form of defeasibility – true/false defeasibility. The second argues against this defeasibility by arguing against any *significant* defeasibility. On both accounts critics would be mistaken if they advanced their interpretations as ordinary statements.[7] In the next two chapters I deal with arguments of the first kind, in particular, with those offered by Joseph Margolis and Robert Matthews. The purpose of my discussion of these two philosophers' positions (an extended discussion of one of them) is not merely the negative one of discrediting certain current arguments against one very important thesis I wish to defend – the thesis tht true/false defeasibility is in principle possible for interpretive remarks. What will also emerge from the discussion are positive, more general, positions on several important issues in critical interpretation.

In this chapter, for example, I discuss whether interpretations can be true, and in this context the role of artistic intention is considered. I argue that if an interpretation accords with a successfully executed artistic intention, then it is true. But this does not mean, as some might think, either that *only* such interpretations are true or that truth is either necessary or sufficient for an interpretation to be acceptable, I indicate why I believe that neither of the latter two views is correct. In the following chapter I continue this discussion by considering what it is to discover properties in artworks and what it is for a work of art to have properties. These discussions in turn lead to discussions about imaginative schemes, about ways of dealing with incompatible interpretations.

Although I want to shed light on these issues, issues that anyone studying critical interpretation must at some point address, filling in the details of my general positions on all of these issues is beyond the scope of the discussion. As I indicated earlier, although I believe that rationality and objectivity are possible in interpretive criticism, I also believe that some widely misused contrasts help to obscure what is needed for them. One aim, therefore, of chapters 4 and 5 is to criticize these contrasts by sketching more acceptable alternatives to them. I am not, of course, the first to attempt such criticism and in my discussion I refer to some of these earlier attempts. If the alternatives I recommend are correct, then, as I suggested, interpreting critics need not choose, for example, between always attending to artistic intention and never attending to it, between discovering properties in artworks and imputing properties to them, between regarding all interpretive remarks as taking the values 'true' and 'false' and regarding none as taking these values.

While arguments of the first kind are directed against a particular form of defeasibility, arguments of the second kind are directed against any significant defeasibility. I (not uncontroversially) take Stanley Fish and Jacques Derrida to be offering arguments of the second kind, arguments against any significant defeasibility for interpretive remarks, and show in chapter 6 that if they are, then their arguments do not succeed. If this is correct, then I would be warranted in assuming, as I do in chapters 4 and 5, that some sort of significant defeasibility is possible in interpretive criticism. My discussion of these two theorists' positions is limited in scope and essentially polemical.

In chapter 7 I lay out in greater detail a positive account of the kinds of defeasibility that would be available to interpretive remarks if interpretive remarks had any of four distinct statuses, that is, if they were statements, hypotheses, reports of experiences-as, or prescriptions. I then turn to critical practice to see what it reveals about the presence of these statuses and kinds of defeasibility.

If we assume that some sort of defeasibility has not been shown to be in principle impossible, then the question becomes what sort of defeasibility is possible. I shall consider whether interpretive remarks about artworks can be statements taking the values 'true' and 'false'.

Arguments against true/false defeasibility for interpretive remarks in art criticism

Critical interpretations are logically weak in principle

The first position I consider, suggested by remarks of Joseph Margolis in *Art & Philosophy* and in some articles on relativism, claims that there is a kind of interpretation for which the truth model will not do:

> critical interpretations . . . are logically weak in principle . . . the reason these judgments are weak depends . . . on the very nature of an artwork and on the impossibility of providing a principle for demarcating what is and what is not *in* a particular work. If one concedes the point, it becomes quite impossible to show that interpretive judgments *can* be true.[8]

Margolis allows that sometimes when we speak of interpretation in art criticism we may mean merely to emphasize virtuosity with respect to what is describable. That is, some so-called interpretive effort 'may be construed as descriptive – in the sense that what is *hidden in* a work may be disclosed by some exercise of critical virtuosity, and that what is thus disclosed may be truly ascribed to that work'.[9] While such critical 'interpretations' can be true, Margolis is not concerned with interpretations of this kind.

Ruling out the value 'true' for some class of claims while retaining the values 'plausible', 'implausible', and 'false', is said not to be foreclosed on logical grounds alone and, therefore, whether this ruling out has 'a significant use' in a given domain of inquiry is thought to depend 'at least on an analysis of the pertinent properties of that domain'.[10] It is argued that the pertinent properties of art criticism give a significant use to the ruling out of the value 'true' for interpretive claims in this domain.

> [I]nterpretive judgments applied where, in principle, we cannot say with certainty what is and what is not 'in' a given work cannot be confirmed in the strong sense in which, normally, causal claims can be. We are restricted there to appraisals of reasonableness or plausibility . . .[11]

Assessments of critical interpretations of artworks as plausible are, if the position is correct, not as such tentative or provisional since the interpretations are not further assessed in terms of truth. While there is a way in which these interpretive claims can be false, they do not take the value 'true'.[12]

How are we to understand the claim that critical interpretations are logically weak in principle? The text suggests two meanings: (1) interpretive remarks *cannot be true*, or (2) interpretive remarks *cannot be shown to be true*. (2) is a weaker claim, allowing as it does the possibility of the remarks being true, even if the critic could not know that they were.

I shall start by considering the claim understood as (1). If there were some question as to whether Margolis is committed to (1) as well as to (2), then there would be some question as to whether my objections here tell against Margolis. In arguing against (1), however, I shall provide objections which have force also against the claim understood as (2).

The claim that critical interpretations are logically weak is to be understood as *critical interpretations cannot be true*. The argument for this claim depends upon the two factors previously cited – 'the very nature of an artwork' and 'the impossibility of providing a principle for demarcating what is and what is not *in* a particular work'. Let us try to see how these factors might be thought to lead to this conclusion.

We are asked to assume that a (or the) goal of critical interpretation in the arts is to find ways in which the artistic design of a work can be coherently construed.[13] The artwork which is the object of this interpretation is said to have a somewhat peculiar nature – it is at once physically embodied and culturally emergent. That is, although one can identify and refer to an artwork by referring to, or identifying, the physical object in which it is embodied ('Michelangelo's *David* may be identified and referred to as a sculpture embodied in a particular block of marble'[14]), the artwork is not identical with that physical object.[15] While only extensional predicates are needed to talk about physical objects, intensional predicates are needed to talk about artworks, for artworks exist and can be identified as artworks only within a cultural context.[16] Artworks are culturally emergent entities; they exhibit culturally significant properties which cannot be ascribed to the merely physical objects in which they are embodied.

If artworks are culturally emergent entities, then we cannot apply to them 'the usual criteria for demarcating what is and what is not "in" an object'.[17] There can be no formal demarcation line between what is internal to (is in) and what is external to (is outside) these works.[18] The emergent properties of artworks are different in kind from the properties ascribable to merely physical objects: emergent properties cannot be said to be in artworks in the straightforward sense in which physical properties can be said to be in physical objects. Artworks 'lack individuating boundaries that are as clear (at least as relatively clear) as the boundaries of macroscopic physical objects'.[19]

In so far as I understand Margolis' position, we have 'descriptive access' to some of the artwork's properties – the work's describable properties. These properties may be discovered in the work. The work's emergent properties, however, are 'interpretively accessible'. These properties are imputed to the work by interpretations, they are not discovered in it. Which emergent properties can defensibly be attributed to the work depends in part on the culturally determined myths or schemes of imagination that interpretations bring to bear on the work. While some particular facts about artworks are, therefore, independent of the myths or imaginative schemes brought to bear in interpreting them, interpretations are ineliminable because they are responsible for the work's emergent properties.

Interpretations, understood as proposals about how the artistic design of an artwork can be construed, are said to be made from within the perspective of imaginative schemes or myths. If, as Margolis believes, a number of imaginative schemes or myths are admissible, then it is logically possible that 'plural, non-converging, even incompatible' interpretations of the artistic design can be generated.[20] (The interpretations in question here would be genuinely incompatible, however, only if these interpretations took the values 'true' and 'false'.) If, moreover, the only restrictions[21] on what counts as an acceptable interpretation are that the interpretation be 'compatible with the minimally describable properties of the work in question'[22] (interpretations incompatible with these properties can be false) and conform to 'admissible myths or schemes of imagination',[23] then given that these restrictions do not rule out seemingly incompatible yet equally acceptable interpretations for a single work, it is claimed one has good reason to regard these interpretations as taking the values 'plausible', 'implausible', and 'false', but not the value 'true'.

In order to see why these restrictions have this consequence, let us look more closely at Margolis' imaginative schemes or myths. These myths or schemes are admissible for criticism whether or not they are true, for such a scheme or myth is, according to Margolis, a system of ideas 'which, *independently* of the scientific status of the propositions it may subtend, is capable of effectively organizing our way of viewing portions of the external world in accord with its distinctions'.[24] The truth of any given imaginative scheme, therefore, 'need not be presupposed in the critical effort to interpret a work in accord with the perspective'[25] of that scheme. For example, the imagery of Freudian psychology, of Christian religion, of Marxist political theory, can become part of the general culture; the Freudian, Christian, and Marxist myths would then be influential myths, affecting our ordinary habits of thinking and perceiving. It is these kinds of embedded myths or schemes that have relevance for criticism, and they retain their relevance whatever the truth status of the hypotheses which give rise to them. For example, in writing his *Commedia*, Dante relied on Catholicism. If one wants to interpret Dante, one must understand Catholicism. It seems, therefore, that even if Catholicism were false doctrine, one would need to use the Catholic myth to interpret some works. 'We should otherwise have to give up Dante's *Commedia* if we were at once practicing literary critics and anti-Catholics in a broader intellectual arena.'[26]

While Margolis acknowledges the relevance of the Catholic myth to an understanding of Dante's work, he also believes that one cannot logically exclude the relevance of a number of other myths. The appeal to authorial intent as a way to privilege certain interpretations is rejected. '[T]here is', he says, 'no satisfactory way . . . of fixing authorial intent within a work so as to exclude the relevance of changing interpretive schemata',[27] and 'there is no logical reason why, even if authorial intent may be validly ascribed, that a work may not support plural, non-converging interpretations consistently with such intent'.[28] If this is correct, then whatever the relevance of the Catholic myth given Dante's intentions, we cannot logically exclude the possibility of other myths, be they Buddhist, Marxist, Freudian, atheistic, or other. It is, however, in principle possible that one could, using some such myth, produce an interpretation that would, if interpretations took the values 'true' and 'false', contradict the original, while being, like the original, responsible to the particular work and to an admissible myth. Moreover, it is in principle possible for there to be interpretations that would be incompatible if true, yet each of which is consistent with the Catholic myth and authorial intent. If interpretations that would be incompatible if they had to be true when defended were admitted to be jointly defensible – nothing is wrong with any of them (each is backed by equally good reasons, each of them firmly demands acceptance) – then to avoid, as we must, contradictory affirmation, we should regard the interpretations not as statements that can be true or false, but rather as hypotheses which can be plausible, implausible, and false, but not true.

If we regard interpretations in this way, we allegedly stay within the cognitive mode; we avoid the difficulty of joint and contradictory affirmation without switching, as did Stevenson, to an alternative mode such as the imperatival mode. The joint defense of what on a model of truth would be incompatible interpretations requires not only that we adopt a model of plausibility for these interpretations, it requires that the artworks thus interpreted be culturally emergent entities and that there be no principle for demarcating which of the properties ascribed by these interpretations are 'in' the work.

Thus, in outline, the position in question; let us see whether the pertinent properties of art criticism do, as alleged, provide good reason for eliminating the value 'true' for interpretive claims in this domain.

In my discussion of this position, I claim that:

(1) Not all critical interpretations (interpretations understood as construals of the artistic design of a work) are made from within the perspective of a myth, a myth as understood by Margolis.

(2) Myths are not generally admissible for criticism independently of the hypotheses from which they derive.

(3) The sharp contrast Margolis relies on between macroscopic physical objects, with agreed upon criteria for determining what is and what is not in them, and artworks for which such criteria are lacking, is an illusory one. Margolis' belief with respect to many properties that we cannot say of them that artworks straightforwardly have them (i.e., that they are in them) is based on an over rigid construal of what it is for any object, be it a macroscopic physical object or an artwork, straightforwardly to have a property.

(4) There are cases in which we can establish interpretive truth, even in the presence of incompatible rivals. For example, in some cases, although incompatible interpretations may initially seem to have equal warrant, if successfully carried out artistic intent is considered, they do not.[29]

(5) There may be genuinely undecidable interpretive disputes in art criticism. Given that there are multiple and potentially conflicting criteria for an interpretation's acceptability (acceptability is distinct from truth),[30] it is possible using a certain criterion to establish one interpretation as accepable, and by using another criterion

to establish a different, even incompatible, interpretation as acceptable. In such cases, moreover, we may
have nothing more to say about the overall merits of the
individual criteria.

I shall discuss (4) first (this discussion occupies the rest of this
chapter), for if any critical interpretation of the requisite kind
can be established as true, then the claim that critical interpretations *cannot be true* is false. Before discussing intention,
however, I shall make some preliminary remarks about
establishing truth.

If, as Margolis claims, one cannot rule out the possibility that
a work may support seemingly incompatible interpretations, this
does not mean, as Margolis acknowledges, that any given work
must or will convincingly support seemingly incompatible
interpretations.[31] Suppose, therefore, that we find that some
interpretive claims do not have seemingly incompatible rivals.
For example, consider claims such as: '*The Turn of the Screw* is
a story about stories', '*Animal Farm* is about totalitarianism'; 'In
Brueghel's *The Fall of Icarus*, the legs in the water belong to the
drowning Icarus'; '*Emma* is a novel about the way in which
society defines and limits domestic happiness'. Critics whose
competency is not in doubt claim to know these things, and rival
critical remarks have not been provided which, if such remarks
could be true, would contradict these claims to know. If we
assume that these sample critical remarks can be interpretive
remarks – that is, for example, we assume that the critic who
advances them, and claims to know that what they say is true,
can be interpreting *for others* who do not know that what they
say is true – then don't these sample critical remarks, given the
absence of apparently incompatible rivals, show that interpretive
remarks can be true?

The fact that rival claims have not so far been provided does
not rule out the possibility that a rival might be provided in the
future. What if as a matter of fact no rival is *ever* presented?
Would we then have shown that an interpretive remark can,
contrary to the position we are considering, be true? Even if a
claim to know that, for example, *Animal Farm* is about
totalitarianism is never defeated, it does not follow that what is

claimed to be known is true. The ignorance of rival interpretations and the presence of the requisite competency do not
by themselves guarantee truth.[32]

However, we ordinarily allow claims to be established as true
– 'Crows are black', 'The sun will rise tomorrow' – even though
we cannot guarantee that these claims are ideally undefeated
(viz., that there is no possible future in which these claims are
defeated). Are there conditions in art criticism such that, if they
were satisfied, an interpretive claim could be established as true
even though we could not guarantee it to be ideally undefeated?

Suppose, for instance, that one wants to know the significance
of the 'blaze of light' in the following lines from Canto IV of
Dante's *Inferno*:

> We did not cease to go on for his speaking, but continued all the
> time passing through the forest – for such it seemed – of thronged
> spirits; and we had not gone far from where I slept when I saw a
> blaze of light which was enclosed in a hemisphere of darkness.[33]

A critic provides the following interpretation: according to the
Catholicism Dante relied on, there is a light which is natural to
man and will stay with man even given the privation of
sanctifying grace if he remains virtuous. Those pagans 'who did
not sin', and whom Dante will soon meet, have this light – the
light of intellect – although they will not have the light of faith or
glory as does Beatrice.

This interpretation of the blaze of light satisfies Margolis'
requirement that an interpretation provide a coherent way in
which the artistic design of the work can be construed. It relies
upon construing the entire physical journey as a certain kind of
spiritual one, one guided by Catholic ideology rather than, for
example, Buddhist ideology. I see no reason, moreover, to regard
the blaze of light *interpretation* as only a description involving
virtuosity (assuming that such a description cannot be an
interpretation of the requisite kind despite its sometimes being
called an interpretation).[34]

Whether the interpretation proposed is true does not depend
upon whether men in fact have the natural light of intellect, i.e.,
upon whether Catholicism is in this regard correct.[35] The
interpretation is true if in Canto IV the light mentioned is the

light of intellect, whether or not in actual life such a light exists. I shall claim that there is good reason for believing that the light mentioned in the Canto is the light of intellect and that the interpretation of it as such is therefore true. The fact that other cultures, ignorant of Catholicism but having their own myths, might interpret the light differently would not, I claim, tell against the truth of the Catholic interpretation.

Intention

If we allow that an interpretation is possible, however, which apparently contradicts the Catholic one, yet is responsible to the minimally describable properties of the *Inferno* and to some admissible imaginative scheme, then we would seem to have possible interpretations with equal warrant and no non-arbitrary way of deciding between them. We could not in such a case establish the Catholic interpretation as true, for joint affirmation of contradictory claims is not possible.

It is debatable, however, whether the Catholic interpretation and its non-Catholic rival have equal warrant. If it could be established that Dante intended the light in question to be the light of intellect and that he was successful in carrying out his intention, then we could establish the Catholic interpretation as true.

To speak of an artist successfully carrying out his intention is to assume that an artist can intend his work to have such and such features and that he can succeed in giving it such and such features. If, therefore, Dante intended the blaze of light to be the light of intellect, and if he was successful in carrying out his intention, then *in* Canto IV of the *Inferno* the blaze of light *is* the light of intellect. If A successfully carries out his intention to do x, it follows that A does x. In such a case, it would be true that the blaze of light is the light of intellect.[36]

Margolis, however, would have to deny that artists successfully carry out intentions *with respect to the interpretively accessible properties of artworks*, for he maintains that these properties cannot straightforwardly be *in* the work. If those properties which are the result of interpretive ascription (and not the result of virtuosity with respect to what is describable) are not *in* the work in the way physical properties are in physical objects, then given what it is to successfully carry out an intention, the artist cannot have successfully carried out his intention to give the work these properties.[37]

To simply assert, therefore, that there are cases in which artists successfully carry out their intentions with regard to interpretively accessible properties of artworks may well be to beg the question against Margolis. While the overwhelming presumption is in favor of there being such cases,[38] I shall argue that to deny that there can be such cases is not merely counterintuitive, it is unnecessary, for one can explain criticism's tolerance of multiple, even incompatible, interpretations (and everything else relevant that is worth explaining) without this denial. The burden of proof, I maintain, ultimately rests with those who accept this denial. Moreover, the theories that they have offered to explain why this denial is necessary – for example, the theory which argues for the complete semiotic independence of signs,[39] or the theory which gives the receivers of such signs exclusive rights to create their meanings,[40] or the theory which makes artworks culturally emergent entities with special kinds of properties – suffer from internal difficulties.

Margolis acknowledges, if I understand him, that there are cases in which artists can fail to carry out their intentions with regard to the relevant sort of properties. He quotes Lukács' discussion of Balzac's *The Peasants* in order to show that failure of intention is compatible with artistic achievement.

> In the novel . . . Balzac wanted to write the tragedy of the doomed landed aristocracy of France . . . Yet, for all his painstaking preparation and careful planning, what Balzac really did in this novel was the exact opposite of what he had set out to do: what he depicted was not the tragedy of the aristocratic estate but of the peasant smallholding.[41]

Lukács goes on to allude to Balzac's historical greatness despite this failed intent, but the point we are interested in here is that failure of intention is taken as possible. Is it not counterintuitive to assume that where failure is possible, success would not be? If Balzac can fail to write the tragedy of the doomed landed aristocracy of France, why in principle would it have been impossible for him to have succeeded in writing it?

On Margolis' view, an artist can successfully carry out his intention only with regard to properties of a work that are descriptively accessible. While description may require virtuosity, it is not 'interpretation' in its central sense. I see no reason, however, for claiming that interpretation in its central sense is not what is at issue in the Balzac case.

If it is counterintuitive to deny the possibility of cases of successfully executed artistic intent in matters where interpretation is required, then some reason for this counterintuitive denial must be provided. The greater explanatory power of a theory which entailed this denial could be such a reason. I shall try to show, however, that Margolis' theory has no such greater explanatory power. Moreover, the theory itself turns out not to be without its own difficulties.

If there are cases of successfully carried out artistic intent with regard to interpretively accessible properties, then the interpretation that exhibits the artist's successfully carried out intention would be true. I claim that we could know that Dante intended the blaze of light to be the light of intellect in Canto IV if we knew that according to the Catholic myth there was only one light, the light of intellect, that non-sinning pagans could have, and that Dante knowingly utilized the Catholic myth, including this detail of it. If its being the light of intellect is in every other way consistent with what Dante wrote, then we would be in a good position to claim that Dante was successful in carrying out his intention.

If we knew that Dante successfully carried out his intention to make the blaze of light in Canto IV the light of intellect, then the critic who interprets the light as the light of intellect gives a true interpretation. Exhibiting successfully executed artistic intent is sufficient for establishing interpretive truth.[42]

If exhibiting successfully carried out artistic intent is sufficient for interpretive truth, it would not follow that it is necessary. Nor would it follow that truth was the only consideration in choosing among interpertations or even that truth was a necessary condition. I shall indicate why these things would not follow.

That an interpretation exhibits successfully carried out artistic intent and that it is a true interpretation would not preclude the possibility of there being interpretations which truly characterize the work in ways other than the artist intended. As T. S. Eliot remarked:

> One is quite aware that one's knowledge of the meaning even of what oneself has written is extremely limited, and that its meaning to others, at least so far as there is some consensus of interpretations among persons apparently qualified to interpret, is quite as much a part of it as what it means to oneself.[43]

Margolis cites a letter Melville wrote to Mrs Nathaniel Hawthorne about his novel *Moby Dick*.

> Your allusion for example to the 'Spirit Spout' first showed to me that there was a subtle significance in that thing – but I did not, in that case, *mean* it. I had some vague idea while writing it, that the whole book was susceptible of an allegoric construction and also that *parts* of it were – but the specificity of many of the particular subordinate allegories were first revealed to me, after reading Mr Hawthorne's letter, which without citing any particular examples, yet intimated the part-&-parcel allegoricalness of the whole.[44]

Even if, as he says, Melville didn't intend a given reference, and we accept his avowal as correct, the reference may nevertheless be plausibly attributed to Melville's work, as Melville himself admits. The specific interpretation of the significance of 'Spirit Spout' given by Mrs Hawthorne provides, on my view, a true characterization of this part of Melville's work, and yet it is not a characterization he intended.

I have been relying here on what I take to be an uncontroversial truth, namely, that there are many ways of correctly characterizing an action, not all of which will exhibit or accord with the way the action was intended. An intention supplies a description of what happened, a description which the agent could normally give of what he was trying to do. Artists in creating works do something, they are agents, and what they do is not merely what they intend to do even when they are successful in carrying out their intentions.

If there are cases in which it can be established that an interpretation exhibits an artist's successfully carried out intention, this would not be sufficient for choosing that interpretation over all its rivals assuming none of its rivals exhibit this intent. While such an interpretation may be true, it may also be a trivial or an uninteresting interpretation; it may make the work an insignificant work, or irrelevant to the concerns of its audience.[45]

In selecting among interpretations, it is also not required that the interpretation exhibit successfully executed artistic intent. Not only, as we have seen, may interpretations that do not exhibit such intent nevertheless be true, interpretations that are not true – that not only do not exhibit this intent but conflict with it – may be equally acceptable or even more acceptable interpretations than those interpretations that exhibit successfully carried out artistic intent.

In many cases it is not easy to decide whether there is a conflict with successfully carried out artistic intent. For example, if Shakespeare intended King Lear to be a *tragedy*, and it could be interpreted as one, is it conflicting with that intention to interpret it as a drama of the absurd (or as a comedy of the absurd), if the category 'drama' (or comedy) of the absurd', or an equivalent, was not available to him? Does the fact that we can, as the result of the elimination of tonal centers, speak of Debussy's works as solutions for avoiding tonality conflict with Debussy's intentions if he did not himself think about his music in this way? Did it conflict with Andy Warhol's intentions, given his avowed apolitical stance, to regard his early pop art works as satirical commentaries on American consumerism?

Suppose, however, we can establish a conflict with successfully executed artistic intent; the interpretation in question is not true. Can this interpretation nevertheless be an acceptable interpretation? It seems clear that an interpretation that is not true may, for example, make a work a more successful or interesting or relevant work than an interpretation that exhibits successfully carried out artistic intent; or it may make it a more interesting work than an interpretation that is true[46] but does not exhibit successfully carried out artistic intent. Acceptable interpretations are not limited to true ones just as true interpretations are not limited to interpretations that exhibit or accord with successfully carried out artistic intent.

I suspect Frank Cioffi is right when he claims that the heterogeneity of contexts of interpretation makes a certain generalization about intention not merely difficult but impossible.

> What any general thesis about the relevance of intention to interpretation overlooks is the heterogeneity of the contexts in which questions of interpretation arise. This heterogeneity makes it impossible to give a general answer to the question of what the relevance of intention to interpretation is.[47]

If so, then there may be cases where although only one of two competing interpretations exhibits the artist's successfully carried out intention, we might nevertheless have reasons against counting just this interpretation as true or counting just this interpretation as acceptable. Since I have already discussed a case in which an interpretation that is true is not one that exhibits successfully executed artistic intent, I want now to look at a case where an acceptable interpretation is not a true one.

Let us suppose that we can know that Grant Wood painted a man and his daughter in *American Gothic*. We learn that Grant Wood intended to paint a man and his daughter[48] and that given what he did paint his intention was successfully carried out. We are assuming, contrary to what Margolis would allow, that an artist can successfully carry out his intention with respect to interpretively accessible properties of artworks in order to see whether, if such a case is possible, the truth of the interpretation that exhibits successfully carried out artistic intent would prevent any interpretation that conflicts with such intent from being acceptable. If it did not, if an interpretation's acceptability is distinct from its truth, even on the above anti-Margolis assumption, one could account for critical tolerance of genuinely incompatible interpretations (the interpretations in questions would be statements taking the values 'true' and 'false') while avoiding their joint affirmation as true.

To return to our example, if we know that Grant Wood painted a man and his daughter, is it therefore unacceptable to regard *American Gothic* as a painting of a man and his wife, as the painting is standardly regarded? Assuming that it is not a picture of a man who has married his daughter, if it is true that it is a picture of a man and his daughter, then it is not true that it is a picture of a man and his wife.

That the painting can be so easily interpreted as a man and his wife tells us a good deal about the painting and why it is initially difficult for Wood's intentions to be recognized. Suppose it could be argued that not only does the standard interpretation show us something interesting about the painting, it in fact makes the painting so regarded a more significant or interesting or successful work. Often in art criticism critics want an interpretation which makes the most sense of the work, or which makes it the most significant or the most successful work.[49] In the Grant Wood case, the demand for an interpretation of the latter kind could compete with the demand that the interpretation be true. The demand for a true interpretation here is a demand for an interpretation that does not conflict with successfully executed artistic intent. In the Dante case, in contrast, these two demands did not compete.

We might in the Wood case point to the incommensurability of the two interpretations given the different requirement each fulfills, and leave it at that. That is, if the two requirements – to make the most sense of the work, and to give a true interpretation – are legitimate ones, and cannot be shown to have unequal weight (both are equally important considerations in deciding on interpretive acceptability), then we cannot decide between two conflicting interpretations, each of which satisfies only one of these requirements while satisfying all remaining requirements. We might have a genuinely undecidable interpretive dispute.

We might do as Cioffi does in what I take to be an analogous case – reading Blake's poem about 'dark satanic mills' as expressing Fabian sentiments[50] – and regard the standard interpretation of Wood's painting as a spontaneous adaption of the painting, an adaption that is curious in being initially unconscious and not requiring any physical change in the painting. Although we do not stand in the same relation to the painting 'after changing our conviction as to what he meant to convey as we did before',[51] we may not thereby be moved to give up the standard interpretation. On the other hand:

[I]f the case were one in which the discrepancy between the author's interpretation and the reader's were one as to the very emotions expressed and not just the accompanying imagery our attitude would be very different . . . Frank Harris read A. E. Housman's poem *1887* as an anti-imperialist gibe and the expression 'God Save the Queen' which recurs in it as a sarcastic jeer until Housman revealed otherwise. Thereafter he naturally found it difficult to do so in spite of his conviction both as to the superiority of his interpretation and its greater consonance with Housman's general outlook. ('How was I to know that someone steeped in a savage disgust of life could take pleasure in outcheapening Kipling at his cheapest?')[52]

In certain kinds of cases, the truth requirement may be given more weight than the requirement of making the most sense of the work. In other cases, it may have equal or less weight. That critics want interpretations that satisfy both these requirements create difficulty when conflicting interpretations, otherwise equally defensible, each satisfy only one of them.

I do not deny that there are cases where we have apparently competing interpretations which are consistent with what an author could have intended (assuming authors can intend their works to have such and such features). If authors can fail in their intentions, then, as we have seen, it follows that they can have such intentions. In such cases we may have no way of telling which of the interpretations exhibit, or accord with, or which of them conflict with, what the author did intend (assuming he did intend something). The interpretations may have equal warrant – e.g., they are responsible to the work's describable properties, they conform to admissible myths. Suppose that in such cases, we were not able to establish truth. We were not able to say which of the properties attributed by the interpretations are *in* the work, although some may be *in* it nevertheless. We could, however, plausibly attribute any of the properties to it. If, in some cases of interpreting artworks, we can only claim to know that it is plausible that a work is such-and-such and not that it is true that it is such-and-such, then this is not something peculiar about interpreting artworks. A great deal of intentional human behavior has occurred which was intentionally determinate although no one now knows or can find out the relevant details in question. Just as in ordinary life situations we must figure out what a person did, so we must figure out what an artist did in his work. Often in our figuring out we must be content with something less than (*knowingly*) establishing truth, although we may give true interpretations nevertheless. In the blaze of light case, in contrast, we assumed that it might be possible to know what the author intended and what he successfully carried out. It is in this case, that I claim that one can *discover* the blaze of light to be the light of intellect *in* Canto IV. If one could discover this, then at least one interpretive claim could be established as true.

Since I do not claim that all interpretive remarks must have the same status, if I have shown that one had adequate warrant for calling some interpretations true, this would not mean that one had adequate warrant for calling many or most, or the most interesting or relevant, intepretations true. My claim in this regard is a relatively modest one. However, if I have shown there to be adequate warrant for calling even a single interpretation true, I have shown why it is a mistake to claim either that interpretive remarks cannot be true, or that they cannot be shown to be true.

In this chapter I have argued that exhibiting successfully executed artistic intention is sufficient for interpretive truth. To argue for this is not to argue either for the view that exhibiting such intention is necessary for interpretive truth or for the view that truth is necessary or sufficient for intepretive acceptability. I have shown why I believe neither of the latter two views is correct.

I have also claimed that if one can establish that Dante intended the blaze of light to be the light of intellect in Canto IV, then one can *discover* the blaze of light to be the light of intellect in Canto IV. In the next chapter I want to consider what it is to discover properties in artworks. This discussion will lead to a discussion about what it is for an artwork to have properties, which, in turn, will lead to discussions about imaginative schemes, about ways of dealing with incompatible interpretations.

Notes

1 'Critics' is being used broadly here to include not only the people whose primary function is that of critic but also those people whose primary function is other than that of critic but who nevertheless make critical remarks about artworks.

2 Allen Tate, 'Our cousin, Mr Poe', *Modern Literary Criticism*, Irving Howe ed., (Boston, 1958), 263.

3 Anthony Savile, *The Test of Time* (Oxford, 1985), p. 62.

4 Edward E. Lowinsky, 'The musical avant-garde of the Renaissance . . .', *Art, Science, and History in the Renaissance*, Charles Singleton, ed., (Baltimore, 1970), 118. Lowinsky is referring to Josquin's *Fortuna d'un gran tempo*.

5 E. H. Gombrich, *Art and Illusion* (New York, 1965), p. 371.

6 Cf. Paul de Man's discussion in *Seminology and Rhetoric* of Archie Bunker's use of these words in response to his wife's query about whether he wants to have his bowling shoes laced over or laced under.

7 Philosophers of art frequently accuse critics in the arts of being confused about the nature of their own practice. For example, Joseph Margolis (*Art & Philosophy*), p. 27): 'Critics and historians of the arts readily confuse the logical status of their own comments because of their confusion and prejudice about the nature of what they are commenting upon.' Colin Radford and Sally Minogue, *The Nature of Criticism* (Sussex, 1981), p. 5: 'the way in which critics approach their own activity often suggests that they misunderstand it'.

8 Joseph Margolis, *Art & Philosophy*, p. 160.

9 Ibid., p. 151.

10 Joseph Margolis, 'The reasonableness of relativism', *Philosophy and Phenomenological Research* vol. XLIII, no. 1 (September 1982). Both quotes appear on 96. Cf. also Joseph Margolis, 'The nature and strategies of relativism', typed manuscript, pp. 1–25.

11 Margolis, *Art & Philosophy*, p. 158.

12 Ibid., pp. 120–1.

13 Ibid., pp. 114, 147, 154, 157.

14 Ibid., p. 39.

15 Ibid., p. 39.

16 Ibid., p. 40.

17 Ibid., p. 122.

18 Ibid., p. 147.

19 Margolis, 'The reasonableness of relativism', 96.

20 Margolis, *Art & Philosophy*, p. 151.

21 No further restrictions can be made because of the cultural dimension of artworks and because of the fact that they 'lack individuating boundaries as clear . . . as the boundaries of macroscopic physical objects,' – one lacks a clear consensus about the correct criteria for demarcating those features of artworks that can be discovered in them from those features merely imputed to them.

22 Margolis, *Art & Philosophy*, p. 155.

23 Ibid, p. 159.

24 Ibid., p. 152, my italics.

25 Ibid., p. 148.

26 Ibid.

27 Ibid., p. 157.

28 Ibid.

29 I claim that there are a number of factors to be considered when trying to establish the truth of an interpretation. Exhibiting successfully carried out artistic intent and not conflicting with successfully carried out artistic intent are among them.

30 As I use the term 'acceptable', it can happen that an acceptable interpretation is not a true one. Critics while interested in truth (and hence interested in whether interpretations exhibit successfully executed artistic intent or do not conflict with such intent) are also interested in things other than truth. For example, they are interested in whether an interpretation makes the work a successful work or a significant work. I shall argue that in some cases these latter interests can compete with the interest in truth. I also discuss whether the factors relevant to determining truth can themselves compete.

31 Margolis, *Art & Philosophy*, p. 151.

32 How independent the abilities to assess truth values, to discern properties in the work, and to determine whether rival interpretations have been considered, are of whether what one claims to be true is true, depends upon the position one takes with regard to idealism/realism disputes. If one claims that truth is *not* assured even if a claim to know is ideally undefeated – that is, 'there is no possible future in which the claim to know' – is defeated, then one is advocating a form of realism with respect to truth. If one claims that an *ideally* undefeated claim would be true, then one is advocating a form of idealism with respect to truth. Richard Warner discusses the idealism/realism dispute in 'Subjectivity and objectivity', a paper presented at a New Jersey Regional Philosophical Association meeting.

33 Dante's *Inferno* (Canto IV, lines 64–9) translated by John Sinclair (New York, 1961), pp. 60–3.

34 In chapter 8, I discuss whether interpretations can be descriptions but in that chapter the interpretations considered are statements taking the values 'true' and 'false'. Margolis is claiming here that interpretations are not statements taking the value 'true', and, since descriptions are statements taking this value, interpretations are not descriptions.

35 It does not even depend upon whether Dante believed in Catholicism. T. S. Eliot in *Selected Essays* (New York, 1960), p. 118 says: 'I doubt whether belief proper enters into the activity of a great poet, *qua* poet. That is, Dante, *qua* poet, did not believe or disbelieve the Thomist cosmology or theory of the soul; he merely made use of it, or a fusion took place between his initial emotional impulses and a theory, for the purpose of making poetry.'

36 Barring, of course, successfully carried out inconsistent intentions on Dante's part. In the discussion that follows I shall assume that successfully executed contradictory intentions are ruled out and that the works we are dealing with are consistent works.

37 'There is', Margolis claims, 'no way in which an "autonomous" object – the artwork – can be antecedently identified, so that evidence of authorial intentions can somehow be found directly *in it*.' (*Art & Philosophy*, p. 168) Rather, 'reference to an artist's intention *in* an actually produced work requires locating that work in the wider intentional life of a culture.' (*Art & Philosophy*, p. 167) There are, moreover, competing ways of locating that work within the wider intentional life of a culture, and there may be competing ways of so locating it that are consistent with artistic intention.

38 Critics and artists alike assume that there are cases of successfully executed artistic intent with regard to interpretively accessible properties of artworks. Artists, for example, frequently protest that their works have been misinterpreted, implying that their successfully carried out intentions in the works have not been recognized. Critics accuse their fellow critics of providing interpretations which conflict with possible intended meanings. Among theorists, those who deny that artists' intentions are relevant in assessing interpretive truth or acceptability are not thereby committed to denying that artists succeed in carrying out their intentions. Rather they are committed to the irrelevance of any such successfully carried out intention. That is, it is claimed that even if author A meant x and his work can be read as x, y might nevertheless be a correct or an acceptable interpretation.

39 Cf. chapter 6, pp. 95–105.

40 Cf. chapter 6, pp. 86–95.

41 Margolis, *Art & Philosophy*, p. 178.

42 Assuming, of course, that successfully executed contradictory intentions are ruled out.
43 T. S. Eliot, 'Introduction', to G. Wilson Knight, *The Wheel of Fire* (New York, 1963), p. xviii.
44 Margolis, *Art & Philosophy*, p. 167.
45 In the quotation I cite below from Cioffi, Frank Harris claims his interpretation of a Housman poem would make it a better poem than Housman's own interpretation. In this case, reason is given for not choosing Harris's interpretation over Housman's. In the Grant Wood case I discuss below, there may well be reason for choosing the interpretation that makes it the most successful work over the interpretation that is true.

T. S. Eliot suggests another reason why the interpretation that exhibits successfully carried out intent may not be given precedence over other interpretations. The author, he says, may change his mind about his own work. ('The modern mind', *The Use of Poetry and the Use of Criticism* [London, 1964] p. 130):

> And in one sense, but a very limited one, he (the poet) knows better what his poems 'mean' than can anyone else; he may know the history of their composition, the material which has gone in and come out in an unrecognisable form, and he knows what he was trying to do and what he was meaning to mean. But what a poem means is as much what it means to others as what it means to the author; and indeed, in the course of time a poet may become merely a reader in respect to his own works forgetting his original meaning – or without forgetting, merely changing.

If the author changes his mind about his own work, the work may mean something other than what he originally intended it to mean. The change of mind can take different forms. Brecht's change of mind about the nature of Galileo's recantation – what he originally thought was justifiable was later condemned as a major crime – required him to rewrite his play *Galileo*. The change in mind suggested by Eliot is more like the spontaneous adaption of a work that Cioffi describes. The author without changing a word in the text changes its meaning. An author might be tempted to change his mind about the work if the work became a better work under a different interpretation.
46 In this case I am thinking of an interpretation that does not conflict with successfully carried out artistic intent although it does not exhibit such intent.
47 Frank Cioffi, 'Intention and interpretation in criticism', *Proceedings of the Aristotelian Society* vol. 64 (1964), 311.

48 Wood's daughter, the model for the female in the painting, for example, claims that her father took himself to be painting a man and his daughter.

49 It is because the critic in the quotation cited on p. 61 thinks his interpretation makes Housman's poem a superior work that he is reluctant to give it up.

50 Cioffi, 'Intention . . .'313.

51 Ibid., 314. Cioffi is referring to Blake's lyric.

52 Ibid.

5

Status and Acceptability Standard: Discovery, Imaginative Schemes, Incompatible Interpretations

Arguments against true/false defeasibility continued

I believe that Margolis and I disagree about what it is to discover properties in artworks. Although I agree that there is no fixed demarcation line between what is internal and what is external to an artwork, that one often cannot say with certainty what is or what is not in a work, and that we reassess artworks in light of continuing experiences, yet on what I take to be a satisfactory notion of discovery, I see no reason why one cannot discover that the blaze of light is the light of intellect to Canto IV of the *Inferno*. What, therefore, is an adequate view of discovery?

Discovering properties in art works

There is a long-standing debate in the philosophical literature about whether interpreters discover properties in works or only impute properties to them. This debate is frequently carried on in terms suggestive of mutually exclusive and exhaustive positions.[1] However, when one answers what I take to be the requisite and prior question – what is it to discover properties in a work – then, I believe, one sees why discovery and report are not in opposition to, but are bound together with, invention and imputation.

While I hold that it is a mistake to claim, as some theorists do, that imaginative schemes of the sort we have been discussing have no place in interpretive criticism – if psychoanalytic theory, for example, provided a legitimate account of human motivation, then psychoanalytic categories could be relevant in interpretive criticism even if the artist had not known about these categories – I do not believe that it follows from this that one must, therefore, only be imputing properties to the work, not discovering properties in it.

In discussing discovery in the arts, I find the concept of the world of the work to be a helpful one. Using this concept, I shall give a sketch of what discovery involves.

An artist in making a work (in painting, composing, writing, . . .) creates or makes a world, what some have called the world of the work. Critics discover a world, the world already made by the artist. In bringing 'the world of a particular work' to 'consciousness of itself',[2] in discovering the many ways it can be, the critic discovers what classifications the artist has effected, where the 'joints lie'.[3]

However, the best critics can remake this made world, for they effect classifications that reorganize the work's world, which bring out new likenesses and differences in it. Once this made world has been remade, this remade world can influence how one views the ordinary world. Critics, thus, by remaking a made world, by discovering new ways of organizing it, can remake the ordinary world.

One might argue that critics do not remake the world of the work or, as I say even more controversially, the ordinary world, but rather they remake our way of viewing the world, they remake or reorganize our perception of the world rather than the world itself. But how the world is is not independent of how we regard it – the world is all the way our true descriptions say it is. Nelson Goodman, for example, has argued for this way of viewing the issue. My points could be recast, however, in terms of the less controversial thesis, i.e., in terms of remaking or reorganizing our perception of the world.[4]

To illustrate how discovery works: suppose that after reading *Romeo and Juliet*, or *Tristan and Iseult*, readers perceive the ordinary world in terms of romantic love – a love which is immediate and overpowering, which requires 'two people to love each other with every single sense and with their every thought, forever'. Suppose they then read De Rougemont's critical study *Love in the Western World*, where it is suggested that romantic love is a seeking after obstacles.[5] If they then re-read *Romeo and Juliet* or *Tristan and Iseult* in the terms De Rougemont suggests, and if they find that these terms fit, then they may subsequently reconceive romantic love in the ordinary world. Although Shakespeare does tell us that the path of true love never did run smooth, although there are countless obstacles, one might not have seen the *necessity* of their presence. De Rougemont discovers what is there to be found in Shakespeare or Bédier, although De Rougemont's discovery is a creative one. He has effected classifications, but these classifications bring out features in an already made world.

In criticism one can focus on the artist's share – 'In the land he has made, the artist is entitled to everything he wants, if it's there'[6] – and marvel that some artists are able to make such incredibly rich worlds. Or one can recognize the critic's share. One need not claim that everything one finds in a work is something the artist intended to put there,[7] although it may be there nevertheless. One may use terms to characterize a Shakespearean world which Shakespeare would not, or could not, have used. The classifactory language might not have been available. If the language is adequate, then its classifications can be used without anachronism.

If these suggestions about discovering properties are correct, then imputation is not opposed to discovery: rather it is integral to it. As Nelson Goodman points out:

> knowing is as much remaking as reporting... Perceiving motion... often consists in producing it. Discovering laws involves drafting them. Recognizing patterns is very much a matter of inventing and imposing them. Comprehension and creation go on together.[8]

Having properties

Even if artworks were, as Margolis maintains, 'culturally freighted phenomena', and what properties were attributed to them necessarily depended in part on the culturally determined beliefs which critics brought to these works, it would not follow that some of the properties were not in the artworks. I suspect that Margolis holds that many of the properties attributed to artworks cannot be properties the artwork straightforwardly has because he is committed to an unrealistically rigid account of what it is for any object straightforwardly to have a property. Margolis has relied on a sharp contrast between ordinary physical objects, for which he believes there are agreed upon criteria for distinguishing the properties that are in them from those that are external to them, and artworks, for which he believes there are no such criteria. However, it seems doubtful that an ordinary physical object (as opposed to an artwork) is, as suggested by Margolis, given to us so that we simply read off the properties that are clearly *in* it.

We classify both macroscopic physical objects and artworks (assuming, with Margolis, for the sake of the present discussion, that no artwork is identical with a physical object) according to our interests and needs. How we classify affects what properties we take to be *in* an object. An object, for example, a banana, that is yellow in one realm of discourse – a banana is a yellow *fruit* – may be green in another – a given banana may be a green *banana*. A banana is edible. It may (or may not) be a phallic symbol, or responsible for the exploitation of the natives of central America by north American businessmen.

Which properties are essentially in a banana was the subject of a recent report:

> A schoolteacher down the street from me who teaches history and geography at the local lycée uses one textbook that describes bananas as yellow fruits grown by peasants in poor, hot countries for 11.5 per cent of their market value and exported and sold by foreign intermediaries who pocket the other 88.5 per cent. Last week, the teacher had a visit about bananas from an angry mother. The mother wanted the teacher to tell her twelve-year-old son that while bananas were indeed yellow fruits grown in poor, hot countries and sold for a lot of money by wicked foreign intermediaries, the exploitation of banana farmers was not really part of the essence of 'banana'. She had tried to tell him this herself, she said, but he did not believe her. He believed his textbook, which had a page about bananas in a chapter entitled 'The World Today'.[9]

Certain ways of taking objects get entrenched; stable predicates are available to us as well as stable realms of discourse.[10]

We read off the properties of an object when, using a fairly standard set of predicates and operating within a standard realm, we are easily able to determine which from among the alternative predicates we are using apply to the object. People are standardly sorted according to sex and color; given the predicates standardly used in these realms, people are either female or male, white, brown, black, red or yellow. Apples and grass are sorted by color; the former are red, the latter is green. The earth is sorted by shape. If we use the alternatives 'flat' or 'round', the earth is round. If we use 'circular', 'elliptical' etc., the earth is elliptical. There are certain entrenched realms and predicates available to us for use with ordinary objects like apples, and certain ones for use with artworks. Artworks are either paintings, or dances, or plays, or sculptures . . .; plays are either tragedies, or comedies . . . . However, when we use new realms or new predicates with regard to either apples or artworks, decisions must be made about the non-deviancy and projectability of these realms or predicates, as well as decisions about the competency exercised in applying them if one is to establish truth.

The lack of unanimity among critics, the resistance to new interpretations which conflict with entrenched patterns of thought, the desire for novel interpretations, and the always present possibility of error, are features characteristic of the critical realm. They have their parallels in the scientific realm. Such features do not, however make talk of discovery inappropriate in either realm. Lorenz's hypothesis that the ether was stationary, although once reasonably believed to be a discovery, did not prevent later scientists from discovering that there was no ether. While critics cannot discover works simultaneously to have and not have a given property, they can sometimes discover what properties artworks do have, even if this process of discovery never finishes. Moreover, this discovery process is not, I claim, limited to a critic's descriptive efforts.

The truth status of an imaginative scheme

In talking about discovery, I claimed that if psychoanalytic theory, for example, did provide a legitimate account of human motivation, then this theory would be useful in interpreting some artworks. For example, suppose Freud's two essays, 'A special type of object choice made by men', and 'The most prevalent form of degradation in erotic life', described patterns of sexual behavior which fit the behavior of humans in much of Western Culture. If *Adolphe* and *Romeo and Juliet* could be shown to be organized in terms of these patterns, then it seems reasonable to regard the critic doing this organization as discovering properties in these works. These properties need not be ones that either Constant or Shakespeare intended but they could be properties that did not conflict with those intentions.

This suggests, however, that the truth of any given imaginative scheme is relevant to whether the scheme is an acceptable one, and, as we saw, Margolis denies this. Moreover, the Dante example, showing as it did that one has to use the Catholic myth in interpreting the *Commedia*, regardless of the truth of Catholicism, seems to support the latter position rather than mine.

However, although I agree that the Dante example demonstrates that in order to interpret some works one has to use schemes regardless of the truth of the hypotheses from which they derive, this does not show that the truth or falsity of the hypothesis is always irrelevant in assessing the acceptability of the interpretive claim generated in accordance with the related myth. For there is a difference between understanding the imaginative scheme an author uses in a particular work and deciding whether such an imaginative scheme can be used to generate interpretations of all works. The admissibility in general of a scheme for generating interpretations of works does depend upon the truth status of its parent hypothesis, although in particular cases understanding the scheme independently of the truth value may be required.

Using schemes whose imagery derives from systems of ideas which have been shown to be wanting in their disciplines of origin will not provide one with true or otherwise acceptable interpretations, unless the work makes clear use of that scheme. If, for example, it were convincingly argued by psychologists that many of the important claims made by Freudian psychologists were seriously misguided, then an interpretation based

upon imagery from that psychology would be rejected for all
works except those in which the scheme had been explicitly
employed. That is, 'if Freudian psychoanalysis were scrapped as
false science', 'if Empson had wrongly assumed it was true',[11]
then his Freudian interpretation of *Alice in Wonderland* would
lose any critical currency it has. As Francis Sparshott remarks, if
Freudian doctrines 'are rubbish, who cares if they can be
applied?'[12]

If we require a critic's scheme to meet truth standards – it is
'true' if the hypothesis from which it derives is true – what
prevents a competent critic from establishing his interpretive
claim as true if he can show that he has used an adequate ('true')
scheme; that according to that scheme the work is such-and-
such; that he has not failed to consider any rival claim; and that
his interpretation does not conflict with successfully carried out
authorial intention?[13]

In those cases where we cannot know what an author
intended and hence we cannot know whether interpretations
that accord with our true beliefs, with our true imaginative
schemes, conflict with authors' successfully carried out intentions,
the inclination to regard these interpretations that accord with
true beliefs as true is strong (assuming these interpretations are
otherwise satisfactory). Sometimes, however, one must be
content with establishing plausibility, for one might have two
competing interpretations which accord with one's true beliefs,
which make the work as successful a work, and which to an
equal extent fulfill the other truth conditions.

I have said that being responsible to general truths about
religion, society, and so on, that is, using true imaginative
schemes, is a relevant consideration for truth. The imaginative
schemes of the sort we are discussing are true if the hypotheses
from which they derive are true. But can we show that schemes
such as the psychoanalytic, the feminist, etc., are true? If the
hypotheses from which such schemes derive attempt to provide
'true' accounts of some 'sector of the world',[14] then I see no
reason why in principle we cannot do so. Given that there are
alternative hypotheses and that no Archimedian point exists
outside the hypotheses from which to judge the relative merits of
each, it will often be a difficult task to decide which among

competing hypotheses is to be established. Difficulty is not, however, impossibility. We might, for example, have to consider the hypothesis' consistency or coherency, its fecundity, its simplicity or its utility, for these factors, rather than being supplemental to truth, are often used as tests for it.[15] The scheme whose hypothesis was established as true would thus be true.

The use of an imaginative scheme

Although in interpretive criticism critics approach works with different conceptual frameworks, not all critics come to their task with large scale schemes of the imagination originating in disciplines outside criticism. Some come with systems of organization provided by a critical methodology – historical criticism, genre criticism, reader response analysis, and so on. Some of these latter categorizations or schemes do not have truth values, and here Margolis and I would perhaps agree, for the critic who proposes them can best be understood not as making a statement or advancing a hypothesis, but as proposing a way of organizing a field of inquiry, a way he believes will contribute to an understanding of the objects so organized.[16] Arguments for a categorization or scheme of this sort would not, therefore, be in terms of the categorization's truth; rather they would be in terms of the categorization's efficacy in furthering understanding.[17] If genre criticism, or reader response analysis, is a categorization of this sort, then it would be justified by showing how it contributes to an understanding of the works organized in terms of it. For example, one could show how attending to the 'reader's response to the words as they succeed one another on the page'[18] could further one's understanding of these words. Consider Shakespeare's:

> Now is the winter of our discontent
> Made glorious summer by this sun of York;[19]

If the reader stops at the end of the first line he expects the speaker to be in a state of discontent, which expectation is defeated when he reads through to the semicolon. Moreover, in hindsight, the reader can see that his original expectation, though defeated initially, is, in a sense, ultimately satisfied, given the events of the entire play.

If there are right and wrong categorizations here, even if not true or false ones – right categorizations would be those whose categories were projectible rather than non-projectible, non-deviant rather than deviant – unless a critic uses a right categorization he could not claim that the interpretation he gives using the category is correct (unless the artist had had the categorization in question in view as he worked). Once a scheme of organization is in place, critics can make assertions using the categories it provides. *Waiting for Godot* is a drama of the absurd, *Adam's Rib* is a comedy of remarriage. If the factors I have mentioned are relevant in determining truth, then what prevents some of these claims from being established as true if the relevant factors have been met?

Sometimes a critic comes to his task with a less articulated set of beliefs – beliefs which may or may not be sorted out or given a distinctive label. The critic who says that Willy Loman is self-deceived about going to Alaska with his brother comes to the work with some beliefs about self-deception, although not necessarily with any large scale systematic scheme or specific critical methodology. What prevents this critic from establishing his claim as true? If it can be established that a non-fictional person is self-deceived, why can it not be established that characters in fiction are so, assuming that the characters in such fictions are to be understood as representations of people? That some works do not provide enough evidence to establish the truth of interpretive claims about them may well be true. However, why couldn't other works provide sufficient evidence? Is there something peculiar about artworks such that the evidence they provide is *never* sufficient for establishing the truth of an interpretive claim about them?

Critical interpretations are typically neither true nor false

Robert Matthews suggests that there is something peculiar about artworks, but, unlike the position just considered, his position is not that it is conceptually impossible for interpretations to be true. Rather, any peculiarity here is a contingent matter. Interpretive claims in art criticism, but not elsewhere, are, as a general rule, radically underdetermined by the evidence available, and therefore they are typically neither true nor false.[20]

Matthews' argument depends upon limiting the evidential base upon which the critic can rely.[21] Only so-called internal evidence, evidence provided by the work itself, will be relevant. External evidence is excluded. 'Interpretations in art criticism are normally construed, and properly so given the purpose of art criticism, in such a way as to render "external evidence" (i.e., evidence not provided by the interpreted work) irrelevant. Thus, for example, there is no external evidence that would decide the truth or falsity of the statement that the governess saw, rather than imagined, the ghosts of Miss Jessel and Peter Quint – at least none that a critic would accept.'[22] If the only evidence that a critic can use is internal, and a critic who offers an interpretation 'typically knows all relevant evidence bearing on his interpretation',[23] and yet he is not in a position to know that the statements constituting his interpretation are true, then it follows that the evidential base provided by the work must be insufficient for establishing truth.[24]

I believe that Matthews' argument rests upon a number of dubious assumptions. Even if one could make the distinction between internal and external evidence clear (and various writers including Margolis have shown why there are serious problems in doing so), it is not evident that external evidence would be irrelevant. I do not understand, moreover, why the purpose of art criticism provides, as Matthews supposes it does, an adequate reason for excluding external evidence. Bertrand Russell's *Autobiography*, Henry James's non-fiction, *English Hours*, are, as Hancher points out, literary works, yet external evidence would seem relevant to interpretive claims about them.[25] External evidence was obviously necessary for the fellow of a Cambridge college who failed to appreciate the irony of Daniel Defoe's *The Shortest Way With the Dissenters*.[26]

If the evidential base is not limited in the way Matthews suggests, is it plausible to claim that a critic frequently knows all the relevant evidence that will bear on his interpretation? If what evidence is relevant depends upon the state of the art, the state of criticism, and the state of the general intellectual climate,[27] then one never knows all the relevant evidence. Moreover, is it clear that as a general rule the evidence is insufficient for establishing truth? Isn't *Animal Farm* about totalitarianism? Aren't those Icarus' legs in Brueghel's painting? Even with regard to claims such as: in Roger van der Weyden's *Three Magi*, an apparition is seen in sky – where a clear rival is readily available (why not a real child seen in the sky?) – it is not evident that Panofsky cannot show that this rival can be ruled out. For example, he argued that the work is a realistic work, and in such a work an apparition, but not a child, could be suspended in space with no visible means of support.[28]

Although I have been arguing that an interpretive claim *can* be true (therefore, it is not true that interpretive claims *cannot* be true), there are many reasons why in particular cases it may not be possible to establish a given interpretation as true. For example, choosing between alternative and competing schemes, schemes which can either be true or right, deciding what the general truths are about life, society, etc., are no simple tasks and, insofar as interpretations are responsible to these general truths or schemes, the difficulty in deciding among the former will be reflected in the difficulty in deciding among the latter. This difficulty, however, of establishing a given interpretive claim as true does not show that the claim cannot be true.

Ways to deal with incompatible interpretations

I have argued that interpretations, when statements, can in principle take the values 'true' and 'false'. If they can do so, then in the presence of incompatible interpretations the critic has several choices. I have already discussed cases in which two incompatible interpretations may not have equal warrant if successfully executed artistic intent is considered. In such a case one of the interpretations may be established as true. I also discussed cases in which the satisfaction of conflicting criteria for interpretive acceptability may make each of two incompatible interpretations acceptable. While only one of the two incompatible interpretations can be true, the other can make the most sense of the work, or make the work a more significant or successful work.

I want now to consider cases in which each of two incompatible interpretations equally satisfies the relevant requirements. Let us suppose that in such cases we do not know what the artist intended, each interpretation uses an admissible scheme (we cannot show that either scheme is not true), each is compatible with the agreed upon properties of the work, each makes roughly the same sense of the work, and so on. In such cases, the critic might nevertheless (1) choose between them, basing his choice on factors such as his overall set of beliefs and desires. Or the critics might (2) regard each as separately plausible or (3) regard each as true relative to its respective scheme.

The critic has sometimes a fourth alternative – he can reject both. He might do this if he could provide another interpretation which accounts for what is taken to be evidence by the earlier views but does not lead to incompatible stances. For example, a controversy has centered around the word 'spare' in the following lines from Milton's twentieth sonnet:

> He who of those delights can judge, and spare
> To interpose them oft, is not unwise

Two readings have been proposed for 'spare' – 'leave time for' and 'refrain from'.[29] If we understand 'spare' in the first way, ' "those delights" are being recommended – he who can leave time for them is not unwise'. If we read 'spare' in the second way, 'they are subject of a warning – he who knows when to refrain from them is not unwise'. The readings offer what appear to be contradictory advice: a person cannot simultaneously refrain from and yet indulge in these selfsame delights. Instead of choosing between these readings, or regarding each as separately plausible, a critic has proposed a third reading which makes choosing between the earlier two unnecessary. 'The lines', he claims, 'first generate a pressure for judgment – "he who of those delights can judge" – and then declines to deliver it; the pressure, however, still exists, and it is transferred from the words on the page to the reader (the reader is "he who"), who comes away from the poem not with a statement, but with a responsibility, the responsibility of deciding when and how often – if at all – to indulge in "those delights".' On this third interpretation, we do not have to choose between two readings of 'spare', for the ambiguity of 'spare' is intended, and its function within the poem can be explained. That is, the ambiguity of 'spare' is assigned a significance in the context of an expectation for judgement. It disappoints this expectation, 'and transfers the pressure of judgment to us'.

Or consider: Pamela is a virtuous virgin, or Pamela is a crafty hypocritical girl. Rather than regard these as incompatible assertions, one might try to show how being a virtuous virgin in certain circumstances requires a measure of craft and hypocrisy.

This fourth alternative is, however, not on a level with the first three. The first three alternatives embody different theories about what to do with incompatibility, while the fourth alternative is something one could do, where conditions allow it, whatever one's theory of incompatibility. I shall look at the first three alternatives.

If a critic takes alternative (3), i.e., he regards the two contradictory interpretations as each true relative to its respective scheme, he resolves the conflict. In so doing, however, he gives up stating either of the two.[30] That is, suppose Brecht says: The plebians in *Coriolanus* are not comic and pathetic types.[31] A bourgeois director insists: The plebians in *Coriolanus* are comic and pathetic types. Assume that both statements have roughly equal textual support, and that neither the bourgeois scheme nor the Marxist scheme can be shown to be false. If we relativize the conflicting interpretations to their respective schemes – e.g., according to a Marxist scheme, the plebians in *Coriolanus* are not comic and pathetic types, according to a bourgeois scheme, the plebians in *Coriolanus* are comic and pathetic types, and each we claim is true within its appropriate scheme – we have gained compatibility. We have done so, however, only because neither of the relativized claims is stating any longer that the plebians are either pathetic and comic types or not pathetic and comic types. If we add a clause to each of the relativized claims to the effect that what each scheme says is true, then we recapture the sense of the original statements. But in that case relativizing no longer fulfills its purpose, for the claims once again conflict.

Some critics are not always content to take the second alternative, to regard the two incompatible interpretations as separately plausible – each is plausible given the evidence available – for it is not merely a matter of considerable intrinsic interest to them which interpretations a work can logically support. These critics use interpretations in their structuring of the ordinary world. Since this world is governed by the law of non-contradiction, opposing interpretations cannot jointly be used to structure it. For example, a critic who is trying to understand certain kinds of human relationships might choose between reading *Pamela* as a story about a virtuous virgin, or as a story about a crafty hypocritical girl (assume here that being a virtuous virgin is not compatible with being a crafty hypocritical girl). On such an occasion and in the absence of knowledge of what the author did intend and successfully carry out, the critic's overall set of beliefs and desires will affect which one of the opposing interpretations he will choose. If, however, a critic believed it was helpful to think of certain kinds of human relationships as ambiguous, or think of them in an ambiguous way, then choosing between them would not be required.

Sometimes the creator of an artwork will encourage critics to view the work in contrasting ways. For example, in Martha Graham's *Rite of Spring*, one of the dancers in the role of the young girl to be sacrificed 'was a fighter, racked with defiance and terror until the end', while another dancer in that role was 'dazed, more quivering'.[32] Graham presumably authorized both dancers' conceptions. In contrast, Beckett corrected a critic's characterization of the Protagonist in his play *Catastrophe*. The critic had written that the Protagonist looked at his audience in abject supplication. The critic relates that he was told by Beckett that it was not Beckett's intention to have the character make an appeal to the audience. Rather, in the critic's words, 'he is meant to cow onlookers into submission through the intensity of his gaze and of his stoicism . . . he is a triumphant martyr rather than a sacrificial victim – a far more pointed political and spiritual statement'.[33]

A critic will take the second alternative – that is, he will regard incompatible interpretations as separately plausible – if he believes that there is no way of determining which of the two is preferable:

> We shall never know for certain whether, for example, Watteau's masterpiece, *L'Embarquement à Cythère* displays its triste and ephemeral eroticists leaving, or leaving *for*, the Isle of Love – either reading being consistent with the language of the title but each requiring a different reading of the work which in view of its ambiguity occupies a limbo of indeterminacy.[34]

In this chapter I have sketched what I believe to be satisfactory accounts of what it is to discover properties in artworks, what it is for artworks to have properties, what role imaginative schemes play in interpretive criticism, what ways there are of handling incompatible interpretations. Such accounts would displace those currently used to support the claim that interpretive remarks cannot be, or the claim that they are not, ordinary statements.

If, as I have maintained, some interpretive remarks could be ordinary statements, then they would be subject to certain kinds of defeat. Before looking at the kinds of defeasibility that are appropriate to such statements (chapter 7), I consider (chapter 6) whether there are other grounds for denying significant defeasibility, and hence for denying the defeasibility appropriate to ordinary statements, to interpretive remarks.

Notes

1 Monroe Beardsley, for example, was critical of those who like Joseph Margolis suggest 'the literary interpreter, too, has a certain leeway, and does not merely "report" on "discovered meaning" . . . but puts something of his own into the work . . .' *The Possibility of Criticism* (Detroit, 1970), p. 40.

2 Stanley Cavell, *Must We Mean What We Say?* (New York, 1969) suggests 'one mode of criticism . . . can be thought of as the world of a particular work brought to consciousness of itself'. That the world of the work, for fictional works, does not exist is, to borrow Cavell's words about the world on the silver screen, 'its only difference from reality. (There is no way, or set of ways, in which it

differs. Existence is not a predicate.)' Although the ontological issues are not settled by these cryptic remarks, such issues are beyond the scope of my discussion.

3 Laurence Foss, 'Art as cognitive: beyond scientific realism', *Philosophy of Science* no. 38 (June 1971), 241. The best artists are the makers of the ordinary world in the 'sense not only of carving it at its joints but of prescribing where its joints lie, establishing paradigm-induced expectations for the rest of us'.

4 I talk about critics making works or worlds of works in 'What is the matter?' *Philosophy and Literature* vol. 1 no. 2 (Spring 1977), 209–21. I am assuming that fictional worlds can have relevance to the actual one. One need not, of course, assume that a fiction says anything directly about the actual world in order for one to learn things from it which one can apply in the actual world. A fictional conversation may be an example of a set of soliloquies in search of audiences. One may then discover numerous examples of this kind of conversation in the actual world.

5 Denis De Rougemont, *Love in the Western World* (New York, 1969).

6 Stanley Cavell, *Must We Mean What We Say?*, p. 233.

7 Ibid., pp. 235, 236.

8 Nelson Goodman, *Ways of World Making*, (Indianapolis, 1978), p. 22.

9 Janet Kramer, 'Letter from Europe', *New Yorker* (28 February 1983), 111.

10 Cf. Mark Sagoff, 'Historical authenticity', *Erkenntnis* no. 12 (1978), 83–93, and Nelson Goodman, 'Reply to Sagoff', in the same issue, 166–8. Cf. also Nelson Goodman's *Languages of Art* (Indianapolis, 1968).

11 Margolis, *Art & Philosophy*, p. 147.

12 Francis Sparshott, *The Theory of the Arts* (Princeton, 1982), p. 257.

13 A question, however, can be raised about whether these truth considerations themselves conflict. Consider an author who, in writing a novel, uses framework C, a framework in which doing p, q and r is sufficient for a female's full development. In the novel, the author has the female character do p, q and r, intending thereby to give us a novel about a fully developed female character. Suppose, however, that framework F is true and framework C is not true. According to F it is not sufficient for a female's full development to do only p, q, and r. Has the author successfully carried out his intention to write a novel about a fully developed female character? Can the character in that novel be fully developed given the framework the author uses, even though any female counterpart in

the world would not be? If the author had used an F framework in writing the novel, then the character would not be fully developed, but the author did not use this framework. Does according with one's true beliefs, in this case according with framework F, compete with not conflicting with successfully carried out artistic intention?

It seems that according with a true imaginative scheme can conflict with the imaginative scheme the artist had in view while he worked. Such considerations give rise to thinking of a fiction as 'a story told by a storyteller on a particular occasion . . . Different acts of storytelling, different fictions. When Pierre Menard retells *Don Quixote*, that is not the same fiction as Cervantes' *Don Quixote* – not even if they are in the same language and match word for word'. David Lewis, 'Truth in fiction', *American Philosophical Quarterly* vol. 15, no. 1, (January 1978), 39.

14 Margolis, *Art & Philosophy*, p. 148.
15 Goodman, *Ways of World Making*, pp. 120–5.
16 Ibid., p. 129.
17 Ibid.
18 Stanley Fish has called attention to the reader's response.
19 *King Richard III*, Act 1, Scene 1.
20 Matthews, 'Describing and interpreting . . .', 5.
21 Richard Wollheim in 'A review of Stanley Fish, *Is There A Text in This Class?*, *New York Review of Books* (17 December 1981), notices a general trend which he labels positivism; 'an evidential base is chosen which is miserly in the extreme but is held to be all that experience warrants'.
22 Matthews, 'Describing and interpreting . . .', 12–3.
23 Ibid., 12.
24 Ibid.
25 Hancher, 'Afterwords', 485.
26 E. D. Hirsch discusses this example in *The Aims of Interpretation* (Chicago, 1976), p. 24.
27 Richard Wollheim, *Art and Its Objects* (New York, 1968), pp. 76ff.
28 Erwin Panofsky, *Studies in Iconology* (New York, 1972), pp. 9–10.
29 Stanley Fish, 'Interpreting the variorum', *Is There a Text in This Class?* (Cambridge, 1980). All the quotes in the following paragraphs are from 149–52.
30 Goodman, *Ways of Worldmaking*, p. 112. The points in the paragraph that follows are made in Goodman's essay.
31 Bertolt Brecht, 'Study of the first scene of Shakespeare's *Coriolanus*', *Brecht on Theatre*, John Willett ed. (New York, 1964), 252–65.
32 Anna Kisselgoff, 'Graham's "Rite of Spring" is a creative triumph', *New York Times* (11 March 1984), 36.

33 Mel Gussow, 'Beckett distills his vision', *New York Times (31* July 1983), 3.
34 Arthur Danto, 'Deep interpretation', *Journal of Philosophy* vol. LXXVIII, no. 11 (November 1981), 692. There are, of course, many cases in which the ambiguity may be intentional. Consider Heinz Politzer's comment about Kafka's *A Commentary* in *Franz Kafka: Parable & Paradox* (New York, 1962), p. 8. 'Whoever intends to extract an unequivocal meaning from this story will, like the man who is its central figure, hear a question instead of an answer. The policeman's "Give it up!" is also spoken to all those interpreters of Kafka who seem to assume that he believed in the existence of only one way leading in one direction to one aim.' Whether the ambiguity is intentional or not, a resolution may not be possible. Consider Auden's 'Musée des Beaux Arts' and William Carlos Williams' 'Pictures from Brueghel II Landscape with the Fall of Icarus'. Auden sees 'how everything turns away' from the disaster in Brueghel's painting while Williams sees how the splash went 'quite unnoticed'.

6

Status and Acceptability Standard: Interpretive Communities, Deconstruction

In chapters 4 and 5 I assumed that some sort of defeasibility was in principle possible for interpretive remarks, that critics were not radically mistaken about the nature of their own practice if they believed that interpretive remarks were significantly defeasible. I maintain that some recent theorists would deny that this assumption was warranted. In this chapter I argue that if, as I suggest, Stanley Fish and Jacques Derrida are claiming that no significant defeasibility is possible for interpretive remarks, then neither has succeeded in showing that this claim is correct. As I indicated earlier, my discussion of their positions is both narrowly circumscribed and primarily polemical.

Arguments against any significant defeasibility for interpretive remarks in art criticism

Interpretive communities

I initially restrict myself to critical interpretations of literary works since the position I shall consider first is advanced by the literary critic Stanley Fish. Fish sets the terms of the discussion by positing two alternatives as mutually exclusive and jointly exhaustive. Either literary texts are self-subsistent repositories of meaning responsible for the experience readers have of them – on this view the meaning of a text remains invariant over time – or literary texts are the end-products of reading experiences, objects themselves constituted by such experiences and not antecedent to them.[2] Fish then argues that the latter alternative is the correct one. If it is, the text as an unchanging object, an object which has the same fixed meaning over time, disappears, and attention is re-directed to readers. Readers who constitute texts come to their task equipped with certain strategies. Using these strategies, interpretive strategies that are fostered and shared by interpretive communities (a single interpretive community consists of those who share the same interpretive strategy), these readers produce interpretations. It is their interpretations that constitute texts, that give texts meanings.[3]

Since there is no upper limit to the number of interpretive strategies readers can use or to the number of interpretive communities that can exist, any given text can in theory acquire an unspecifiable number of meanings.[4] In an earlier formuation of his position ('Interpreting the variorum'), this is not what Fish claims to believe would happen. Rather he claims that an unspecifiable number of different texts would be produced. However, according to a later formulation ('Normal circumstances . . .'),[5] a text can, for Fish, remain the same, even though what is in it can change as different interpretive strategies are brought to bear. The meaning of 'text' shifts from (a) a combination of a particular arrangement of words in a language with some single meaning that has been given to the arrangement (the same particular arrangement of words can be given different meanings, but each arrangement in combination with its distinctive meaning constitutes a separate text), to (b) a particular arrangement of words in a language, where the arrangement has been given one or more meanings (different particular meanings can be given to the same text on different occasions).

As I understand Fish's position, although it is in some respects similar to the position that interpretive remarks are reports of special kinds of experiences, it is importantly different from it. For Fish, interpretive remarks do report readers' experiences but, as will soon be evident, these experiences are thought to be responsible for what properties a work has. In contrast, on the other position, what properties a work has can be ascertained independently of one's experiences-as, and what these properties are affects what it can be experienced-as, viz., what its aspects are. For example, if one isn't adequately aware of the object's properties, one can't be in an appropriate position to have relevant experiences-as.

Fish's properties, to be sure, are different from the properties recognized by the other position. It might be said that whereas the other position countenances properties and aspects, with interpretive remarks being about the latter, Fish's position only countenances properties, but properties that behave more like the 'aspects' of the other position than like its 'properties'. One cannot, however, simply assimilate Fish's properties to aspects, for aspects are contrasted with properties, and there is, as we shall see, nothing to contrast Fish's properties with.

In order for interpretations and the readers' experiences responsible for them to be defeasible, it must be possible to articulate what would count as defeating them. If we think of defeating in terms of providing some sort of evidence against, it must be possible to articulate what would count as evidence against these interpretations. If nothing could in principle count as evidence against them, assuming we think of defeating in the terms I suggest, they could not in principle be defeated.[6] Why might one believe that nothing could count as evidence against an interpretation?

Suppose one believes, as does Fish, that 'the interpretation determines what will count as evidence for it, and the evidence is able to be picked out only because the interpretation has already been assumed.'[7] The interpretive strategy used to produce an interpretation is responsible for what counts as evidence for the interpretation. Suppose further that there are no facts of the matter which are themselves independent of the strategy, but rather it is the strategy itself that determines what the facts which can serve as evidence are. That is, the strategy determines not only what types of facts are capable of serving as evidence; it also determines what we have in a given case by way of particular facts belonging to the type. 'The interpretation constrains the facts rather than the other way around and also constrains the kinds of meaning that one can assign to these facts.'[8]

Consider two readers confronting Milton's *Samson Agonistes*. The first reader claims that *Samson Agonistes* is about Christ.[9] The second reader denies that it is about Christ, citing as evidence for his denial the absence of any reference to Christ. But whether the absence of any reference to Christ is evidence for the second rather than the first interpretation depends upon the strategy one employs. If one uses the strategy of typological interpretation ('Typology is a way of reading the Old Testament as a prefiguration or foreshadowing of events in the life of Christ'),[10] 'the absence of any reference to Christ' is 'evidence of Milton's intention to respect typological decorum';[11] hence not merely is it not evidence against *Samson Agonistes* being about Christ, it can be evidence for its being about him. The strategy determines what facts count as evidence and explains why these facts are evidence. The same fact can be cited as evidence for different interpretations, since each interpretation provides a way of explaining the fact that is consistent with it. One might want to say that 'the same piece of evidence will not be the same when it is cited in support of differing determinations of what is in the text.'[12]

But can what the facts are – e.g., that there is an absence of any reference to Christ, or that Samson despairs – be independent of the strategies themselves? According to Fish they cannot, for whether the alleged fact – there is an absence of any reference to Christ – is a fact depends upon the interpretive strategy. A reader using the typological strategy could argue that 'the mention of Samson *includes* Christ and that thus He is no less mentioned than his Old Testament prefiguration'.[13] Similarly, that Samson despairs is 'a determination which is only possible within the prior assumption that the play is Christian and that therefore despairing is something that its characters can reasonably be suspected of doing or not doing'.[14] If the strategy determines not only what facts count as evidence for an interpretation and how they count, but even what these very facts are, then there seems to be no possibility for counter-evidence. But if no counter-evidence for an interpretation is in principle possible, then it follows that an interpretation cannot in principle be defeated.

Although if Fish is correct about how evidence is determined for an interpretation, then it seems that if one works within an interpretive strategy one can never be forced to give up an interpretation by an appeal to evidence (the interpretive strategy by determining evidence in the way described seems to rule out the possibility of there being counter-evidence), Fish writes as if this were not the case. In reply to a critic, Fish claims 'that it would be damaging to a theory if it were unable to account for the possibility of being wrong'.[15] This suggests that on Fish's theory it is possible to say of a reading that it is wrong. If one could say this, then it seems that interpretations could be significantly defeated. I shall argue that given what Fish understands by 'wrong', however, an interpretation cannot be significantly defeated. 'A significant defeat', as I use the phrase, is a decisive rather than a conditional or provisional defeat.

Fish asks under what circumstances a typological critic of *Samson Agonistes* might 'renounce' his own reading. He suggests three circumstances in which such a renunciation might occur – if there were 'biographical evidence (in a letter, perhaps) that Milton did not write with a typological intention', (p. 294) or there was 'the absence in contemporary responses to *Samson Agonistes* of any reference to typological significances', (p. 294) or there was indication that 'in Milton's other works Samson is always treated as a political rather than a theological example'. (p. 294) However, Fish is quick to point out that 'the evidence that would constitute a challenge' to the typological assumptions 'would *be* evidence only in light of other assumptions which could in their turn be challenged'. (p. 294) For example, if the typological critic did not give a 'privileged status to authorial statement', (p. 294) then the aforementioned biographical information would not count against his reading. Similarly, if the critic did not have 'an historical view of poetry's production and reception', (p. 294) then contemporary responses to the work would not be conclusive. Finally, if the critic were, for example, a genre critic and did not believe that an author's work 'was everywhere informed by the same concerns', (p. 295) then he would not find the character's treatment in other works telling. It is, therefore, always logically possible for a typological critic to let nothing count as evidence against his reading, for any evidence is dependent upon interpretive assumptions and these assumptions can, according to Fish, always be challenged. Fish, therefore, claims that 'standards of right or wrong do not exist apart from assumptions but follow from them; they are standards that are decided upon, not standards that decide –

notions *in* dispute rather than notions that settle disputes'. (p. 296)

While Fish maintains that the literary institution at any give time authorizes 'only a finite number of interpretive strategies' (p. 342) and so at any given time at least some readings can be ruled out, a reading is not ruled out because 'the text excludes it'. (p. 345) Rather it is ruled out because 'there is as yet no elaborated interpretive procedure for producing that text'. (p. 345) It is entirely possible, however, that such an elaborated interpretive procedure might at some later time be established. However, if an interpretive strategy is already established, as is the typological strategy, then it is always conceptually possible for a critic offering a typological reading to allow nothing to count as counter-evidence to his reading. If this is always possible than an interpretation cannot in principle be significantly (i.e., decisively) defeated.

My difficulties with Fish's position start early, for I do not accept as exhaustive the alternatives it initially sets up. If the only alternative to texts created by reading experiences were a formalist text, a self-sufficient retainer and transmitter of meanings, which all critics might attend to if they rid themselves of 'quirks of personality, misfortunes of upbringing, environmental, social and political preferences',[16] then the former alternative might well be the decidedly more attractive one. The text seems not to be self-sufficient in these ways, nor is it even logically possible for critics to rid themelves of the requisite quirks, misfortunes or preferences. I doubt, however, that these are the only alternatives.

Fortunately, it is not necessary for the purpose at hand for me to demonstrate that there are other alternatives; all I need do here is show why, even if one accepts Fish's terms and chooses his alternative, it would not follow that an interpretation cannot in principle be significantly defeated. I shall begin by looking at the claim that *an interpretive strategy determines its own evidence.* The position we are considering takes this claim to mean:

(1) An interpretive strategy determines what evidence is and what the facts of the relevant sort(s) actually are.

We saw that this means it determines not only what *types of fact* are capable of serving as evidence, but also what we have in a given case by way of *particular facts* belonging to the type. The claim could, however, as Richard Wollheim suggests,[17] be taken to mean:

> (2) An interpretive strategy determines the *kind of evidence* readers using that strategy can employ; it determines what kinds of things are capable of serving as evidence, what *kinds of things count as facts*.

(2) is a weaker claim. It does not hold that the strategy determines what we have in the way of particular facts in a given case, and its acceptance does not entail the acceptance of (1). Moreover, it is only if one accepts (1) that the thesis of indefeasibility seems unavoidable. I shall suggest why it is a mistake to accept (1). I shall also argue that even if one accepted (1), it would not follow that an interpretation couldn't in principle be significantly defeated. Indefeasibility of the requisite sort is not an unavoidable consequence of (1).[18]

Wollheim has argued, and I am in agreement, that it is a mistake to claim that a strategy determines what is the case, that it determines what we have in a given case by way of particular facts. If this is a mistake, it is, therefore, a mistake to hold (1). He points out that while language fixes the meanings of words, it leaves open the truth of a sentence. Analogously, he argues, while a strategy may fix what kind of evidence is relevant, it leaves open whether the strategy is supported by the evidence.

> A strategy will tell him for instance, that biographical information is inadmissible, or that mythic patterns are of significance, or that favored grammatical transformations are stylistically relevant, or that voice and person are crucial – but what it will not tell him, because it cannot, is what, within the broad limits of admissibility, is actually the case. No strategy can say, for instance, just how the image of the golden bowl figures in James's novel and to what effect, or whether Milton really did prefer deletion to conjunction in his Lawrence poem, or what and where are the actual changes of voice in *Lycidas*.[19]

Wollheim claims, for example, that the strategy does not determine what the actual changes of voice in a poem are, although the strategy may determine that changes in voice, should they occur, would be crucial, would be evidence for some thesis. It is argued, therefore, that whether any changes in voice occur, and what these actual changes are, is independent of the strategy which recognizes such changes as crucial.[20]

To return to our earlier example, is the absence of any reference to Christ (i.e., the absence of any *mention* of Christ) in the play a particular fact about the play only if one subscribes to a certain strategy? If one subscribes to a different strategy, e.g., one introduces a special sense of 'mention' as the typological critic does, so that, if 'the mention of Samson *includes* Christ', Christ is then thus mentioned, is the alleged 'fact' no longer a fact? If there is reason to doubt that the absence of any mention of Christ is a particular fact about the play only if one subscribes to a certain strategy, as I suggest there is, then there is reason to doubt the truth of (1) – to doubt, that is, that the strategy determines the particular facts. In the typological strategy, the notion of 'mention' that is introduced is certainly not a standard one. That is, although New England includes Maine, Massachusetts, Connecticut and New Hampshire, the sentence 'New England borders on New York', doesn't in the standard sense of 'mention' mention Connecticut, even though it may tell us something about it. Are *ad hoc* maneuvers, as this maneuver about mention appears to be, legitimate? Moreover, is despair a category that depends upon a Christian framework as it is claimed, or is the category available to atheists, Muslims and the like? If the category is more widely available than Fish suggests, then that a particular character despairs can be ascertained independently of the typological reading.[21]

If an interpretive strategy determines that grammatical incoherences would be evidence for a disturbed state of mind, can the strategy make grammatical incoherences in a given text? If a strategy establishes what would count as evidence for a particular fantasy, can it make there be such evidence, for example, in *The Mending Wall*? I would answer 'no' to these questions. If the answer is 'no', then the strategy does not do what (1) says it does.

In order, however, to show why 'no' is the correct answer in these cases I would have to show in detail why the picture of how texts acquire meanings presented by the position under discussion is misguided. I shall not attempt this here, for there is a more direct route to my immediate end. That is, I believe I can show that even if one held onto (1), even if one adamantly refused to countenance the possibility of establishing facts and evidence relevant to an interpretation independently of the interpretive strategies used to produce it, it still would not follow that one could not in principle significantly defeat an interpretation. The reason is a simple one – nothing prevents any reader from make a mistake while using an interpretive strategy. Even if strategies did determine what is the case, what the particular facts are, nonetheless, if a person is confused or careless, he may in using a strategy come up with an interpretation that could be defeated in the strategy's own terms. If one argued that interpretations constitutive of texts were those and only those interpretations that were produced by readers *correctly* using the strategy, then, unless one arbitrarily limited interpretations to just these interpretations (i.e., confused 'interpretations' weren't *interpretations*) one could not rule out the possibility of significantly defeating an interpretation, namely, of defeating an interpretation that was not produced by a non-careless, non-confused reader.

Suppose, for example, I use the strategy of psychoanalytic interpretation and look for underlying fantasies in a given work. Suppose further that while I find an anal fantasy in the work, the other members of my interpretive community find an oral fantasy. If these other members could persuade me that I have made a mistake in using the strategy, that I was confused about how it applied or careless in applying it, could they not in principle significantly defeat my interpretation? I see no reason why not. But if there is no reason why they could not, then even from Fish's point of view, it is false to claim that an interpretation is in principle not significantly defeasible. That is, on what follows from Fish's view, communities have some authority over individuals, and if they do, a concept of significant defeasibility can be built on that.[22]

As we saw earlier, Fish discusses another source of authority – 'the literary institution'. According to Fish, at any one time this institution 'will authorize only a finite number of interpretive strategies'. Although it might initially look as if one could build a significant concept of defeasibility on this institution's authority, I claimed that one could not. Consider Fish's example of an Eskimo reading of Faulkner's *A Rose for Emily*. According to Fish, this reading is currently unacceptable 'because there is at present no interpretive strategy for producing it . . . This does not mean, however, that no such strategy could ever come into play . . . '.[23] If, as Fish believes, such a strategy could come into play and be authorized by the literary institution, then an Eskimo reading of *A Rose for Emily* could be acceptable. An interpretation unacceptable at time *t* for the reason Fish gives is not, therefore, an interpretation that is significantly defeated. An untimely interpretation is neither an incorrect nor indefensible nor implausible nor unobeyable interpretation.

The kind of defeasibility that Fish's strategy dependent interpretations are subject to is not, I shall argue, the only kind of defeasibility available in art criticism. While this defeat can be decisive, it is not ultimately an interesting kind of defeat. Later discussion will reveal defeasibilities that are not linked to individual strategies in the manner in which Fish's defeasibility is so linked. I show, moreover, that one of these latter defeasibilities is especially important in explaining the actual interpretive practice of critics.

Deconstruction

The next position I discuss also calls for revisions in our thinking about texts, meanings, and interpretations. Since the position aims to undermine our belief in the possibility of understanding what any text means – where by 'understanding what a text means' is meant 'understanding *the* determinate meaning of a text or a meaning *privileged* by the culture or tradition' – I am, according to the position, engaging in a self-defeating enterprise when I attempt to understand the position. For when I attempt to understand it for present purposes, I attempt to understand what certain texts mean (i.e., those texts which state the position); I suppose these texts have fixed and invariant meanings, meanings which have special weight or 'truth'. *Ex hypothesi*, however, I must always fail in any attempt to understand a text in this way, and hence, to understand these specific texts. In the spirit of the position, therefore, one may regard the following discussion of it as issuing from the 'free play of signification' initially opened out by the signs in some of Jacques Derrida's texts. The discussant is aware, moreover, of the alleged lack of security in such play.

In my explication of Derrida that follows, I make use not only of some of Derrida's own texts, but of some of the texts which comment on his. In particular I make use of Seung's *Structuralism and Hermeneutics*[24] and Abrams 'The deconstructive angel'.[25]

As I understand the position, texts are signs that are essentially semiotically independent.[26] Texts, moreover, are not limited to written signs, to literary texts, for pictures, films, dances, etc., constitute texts. Indeed, as I indicate below, 'text' is at times used so broadly that nothing remains outside it.

Semiotic independence of the signs that are texts entails independence on a number of counts. Texts are independent of all of the following: individual authors; collective authors or the context of production; readers (individual and collective); the objects of signification, the outside the language referents.[27]

To be semiotically independent is to be able to function as a signifier, as a sign that stands for something, in the absence of, or in separation from, all of the above. A sign independent on all of these counts can function as a signifier. How? Since Derrida has written extensively about literary texts or signs, I shall concentrate first on these.

Literary texts are made up of marks on paper, marks that have already been written – 'un text déjà ecrit, noir sur blanc'. These already written marks function as signifiers in virtue of their ability to retain the past, for these marks are 'traces'. A trace is a remainder of something that is already absent. Its function of standing for something no longer there is its function of substitution or supplementation. But to stand for something that cannot itself be present is not only to retain the past, it is also to efface it, for to be past is to be effaced. Moreover, although traces are traces of something, they are not traces of some original, rather a trace is a trace of a trace which is, in its turn, a trace of a trace *ad infinitum*.[28] Signs for Derrida signify other signs.

Abrams suggests that a trace 'functions as a kind of "simulacrum" of a signified presence'.[29] It is an illusion, however, to suppose that something was ever immediately present, or that something was ever immediately present to itself, for example, that a writer was ever immediately present to himself, that he could know exactly what he meant and transmit that meaning in his writing, that he could, therefore, be the origin and guarantor of meaning.[30] Traces always work in the absence of any such transcendent presences. 'Differance',[31] a neologism which Derrida introduces to cover both differences and deferment, sets the play of signification going. The meaning of any sign lies in the relations of difference, its difference from other signs, and its meaning is perpetually deferred, the referent can never be fully present to the signifier. As Abrams observes, when one tries to interpret the significance of a sign or a chain of signs – 'whose self-effacing traces merely defer laterally, from substitution to substitution, the fixed and present meaning (or the signified "presence") we vainly pursue. The promise that the trace seems to offer of a presence on which the play of signification can come to rest in a determinate reference is thus never realizable, but incessantly deferred . . . no sign or chain of signs can have a determinate meaning.'[32]

How are we to understand Derrida as characterized by Abrams? Is Derrida claiming:

(1) A text (a chain of signs) has *no* determinate meaning.
(2) A text has *no one and only* determinate meaning. This could be the case, for example, if the text had indefinitely many determinate meanings.
(3) A text has *no meaning privileged by the culture or tradition*; no textual meaning has a special weight or 'truth'.

Abrams' remarks most naturally suggest that Derrida is claiming (1). If Derrida were claiming (1). then he would be committed to (2) and (3) as well. Not all readers of Derridean texts, however, would agree that Derrida's commitment extends to (1);[33] few, if any, would deny that he is committed to (2) and (3). Since the points I wish to make here apply *mutatis mutandis* to any of (1), (2), or (3), to avoid controversy I shall assume the minimal commitment on Derrida's part, that is, a commitment to (2) and (3).

What Derrida himself acknowledges giving us is a

> text that is henceforth no longer a finished corpus of writing,
> some content enclosed in a book or its margins, but a differential
> network, a fabric of traces referring endlessly to something other
> than itself, to other differential traces. Thus the text overruns all
> the limits assigned to it so far (not submerging or drowning them
> in an undifferentiated homogeneity, but rather making them
> more complex, dividing and multiplying strokes and lines) – all
> the limits, everything that was to be set up in opposition to
> writing (speech, life, the world, the real, history, and what not,
> every field of reference – to body or mind, conscious or
> unconscious, politics, economics, and so forth). Whatever the
> (demonstrated) necessity of such an overrun, such a débordement,
> it still will have come as a shock, producing endless efforts to dam
> up, resist, rebuild the old partitions . . .[34]

Interpreting a text is not to be understood as getting at what the text means, if one understands 'getting at what the text means' as getting at *the* determinate meaning of the text, or a meaning which is *privileged* by something specifiable outside the text, or a meaning which is *correct*. All those who thought that a privileged determinate meaning of a text existed, or that the text had one and only one determinate meaning, but who disagreed with one another as to where to locate that meaning – was textual meaning to be identified with utterer's meaning, the author's intended meaning? with utterance meaning, what the words meant in the context of their production? with word sequence meaning, what the words could mean given the rules of language?[35] with the readers' experiences (either individually or collectively)? – were mistaken.

If a text does not have a single determinate meaning, or a determinate meaning that is privileged by the tradition or culture, can an interpretation of it be defeated in principle? What evidence would count against the interpretation? All the traditional appeals to evidence – that's not what the author intended; that's not what the signs could have meant at the time they were produced; that's not what the signs could mean given the rules of language; that's not what the referent was – are ruled out. If we understand interpreters to be incessantly deciphering,[36] to be teasing out the complexities of differences – differences which are the result of the play, or in-principle-endless movement, among signs which defers the 'arrest' of signification, which defers 'fixing' the relation between this signifier and this signified – then, given that nothing seems to be available that could count against this teasing out, this deciphering, the interpretations that are the results can never be defeated. Are we not in 'a world without error, without truth, without origin, which is offered to an active interpretation'?[37] In such a world all interpretations are essentially indefeasible, none are false, none are true.

While an interpreter so understood has to chart the connection among signs that give rise to his interpretation – the most 'creative' interpretations requiring the most unnoticed or unusual connections – the crucial factor in interpreting here is not 'truth', but critical ingenuity. The critic, if constrained, is constrained only by the intertext, the entire network of texts or language. It is from the intertext that texts take their meanings. The intertext, as well as an individual text, is, moreover, neither static nor stable. Texts are in a perpetual process of interplay, one with another.[38]

If signs are, as Derrida believes, related to each other in language, both at a given moment and through their history, is it possible that some interpretations, understanding 'interpretations' in a Derridean way, do not work? That is, given the assignments of signs that have been made – certain signs, the signifieds, have been assigned to other signs, the signifiers – isn't it possible that a particular assignment of signified to signifier will be foreclosed? Given the room in Derrida's position for cleverness in making hitherto unimagined connections among signs, this sort of defeat, if logically possible, would be difficult to achieve in practice. Even if it were possible to show that an interpretation would not work at a particular time (one could never of course show that it was wrong or false), given that the intertext is in constant flux, it is difficult to see what would prevent an interpretation that did not work at one time from working at another time.

I am not claiming here that 'anything goes' for Derrida once Derrida gives up privileged meaning. If we relativize the claim of 'anything goes' to some particular time t, then I have allowed some meanings may in theory be foreclosed at t. I am claiming, however, that foreclosure at t does not thereby guarantee foreclosure at t_1. To show that an interpretation is unworkable at a particular time is not to defeat that interpretation in a way traditionally thought to constitute significant defeat.

If something like this is Derrida's position, how would Derrida have us understand what he is saying in his text 'Restitution of truth to size . . .?'[39] In it, Derrida discusses Heidegger's and Meyer Schapiro's interpretations of a Van Gogh painting. Meyer Schapiro believes that the picture clearly is of the artist's own shoes, not as he takes Heidegger to believe, the shoes of a peasant. If I understand what is going on,[40] Derrida is saying that both Heidegger and Schapiro would be *wrong* if they attributed the painted shoes to a subject, be it a peasant or Van Gogh, although Derrida wants us to notice that Heidegger is not, as Schapiro takes him to be, interested in the painting itself, in the painted shoes, but in shoes. We are told by Derrida that Schapiro believes credulously that '[s]ome painted shoes can actually belong and let themselves actually be restored to a real, identifiable and nameable subject. This illusion is facilitated by the closest identification between the alleged custodian of the shoes and the so-called signer of the painting.'[41] But if Schapiro is *mistaken* in believing that the painted shoes can be attributed to a referent, then isn't his interpretation (that they are clearly pictures of the artist's shoes), as well as any interpretation which attributes the shoes to a referent, defeated?

If an interpretation is taken in a standard way – as a statement about the meaning of a work (where identifying the referent of an image is part of giving the meaning of the work) – then on Derrida's view it seems capable of being defeated. How? By showing that the person hasn't done what he claims to have done – he hasn't understood *the* meaning, the one and only meaning, or a meaning privileged by the culture or tradition; this is not because the text has some one and only meaning which he fails to see, or could have some privileged meaning incompatible with his which he has failed to consider, but because it has in principle no meaning of the requisite kind. If Heidegger were interested in the painting itself, and claimed it was a picture of a peasant's shoes, he too would be mistaken. Heidegger and Schapiro would be wrong, not because they got the referent of the painted shoes wrong in the sense that some other referent's shoes are pictured; rather they would be wrong because the whole enterprise they would be engaged in, the enterprise of attributing painted shoes to any referent specifiable independently of the work, is wrong. There are no transcendental signifieds.[42] Interpretations, understood as assertions about privileged meanings, can be defeated by undermining their presuppositions, presuppositions of their having a truth value. Indeed any given interpretation is not only in principle capable of being defeated, one can always defeat it. One can always show how it fails to do what it claims to do. That is,

(1) To show that what an interpretation said was false would be to defeat that interpretation.

(2) Any interpretation claims to tell us either that for some one and only determinate meaning, *M*, or that for some determinate meaning, *M*, privileged by the culture or tradition, the text has *M*.

(3) There is no one and only determinate meaning, *M*, of a text; nor is there any determinate meaning, *M*, of a text privileged by the culture or tradition.

Therefore,

(4) What any interpretation says is false and the interpretation is defeated.

Can we regard Schapiro's statement as an interpretation in the Derridean sense of interpretation, that is, can we see it not as a statement about what the work means, about what its referent really is, but simply as the product of Schapiro's deciphering made possible by the opening out of the painted sign – a statement about traces which itself is a trace? If we could, then presumably the product of this deciphering is as good as any other, it is indefeasible (I assume here the requisite critical ingenuity). The fact that Schapiro might not have intended his remark to be regarded in this way cannot be any reason for us against so regarding it, for signs are semiotically independent of their authors. If we adopt the Saussurian model of language according to which meaning is the product of difference, we could perhaps see what Schapiro does as a product of deciphering. The question at this point is whether one should adopt this model.

Derrida takes Schapiro, however, and I would argue rightly takes him not be engaged in Derridean interpretating, but to mean what Derrida takes him to mean, and hence to be liable, if Derrida's theory were itself correct, to systemic defeat of the sort we have described. But, of course, if Derrida's theory were correct could he attach any special weight or 'truth' to the determinate meaning he attributes to Schapiro's claim in the first place? Unless such a meaning has special weight, what Derrida goes on to claim about Schapiro would not show that Schapiro *is* credulous, *is* under an illusion. Derrida's putative criticism of Schapiro can be decisive only if Derrida's theory is not correct. That is, if Derrida's reading of Schapiro is given special weight, i.e., it is the *right* way to read Schapiro, then Schapiro may be under an illusion (if, that is, no assignment of the painted shoes to an outside the language referent is possible). But Derrida's reading, like any reading, cannot be 'right', if Derrida's theory is correct.[43]

Let us try a somewhat different tack. Suppose that Derrida would agree that *if* an interpretation is a statement about *the* determinate meaning of a text, that is, is a statement that a text has a single privileged determinate meaning, M, *then* it could be defeated. Suppose also, however, that Derrida wants to get critics to stop making such statements, since any critic who makes one will never be right. What he wants critics to do instead is to engage in Derridean interpretation, for the interpretations that result from this activity are not similarly subject to the traditional modes of defeat.

That is, if a critic is locked into logocentrism, the metaphysics of presence, then in interpreting a text, he will make statements about determinate meaning, he will state of a text that it has determinate meaning, M, a meaning privileged by the culture or tradition, and his statements cannot be right. It is not that a critic cannot state that a text has determinate meaning, M; he can, for how else could Derrida have his targets? However, if he understands that there is nothing to justify his belief that this determinate meaning is the only meaning the text has, or is a privileged meaning, then this should encourage him to stop making such statements (at least under these descriptions). What he should start doing is engaging in Derridean interpretation, where he need never worry about being right or wrong. He also need not worry about being understood, in the sense of being perceived to have said something with a privileged meaning. Not simply will he not (because he cannot) be so understood by others, since they won't (because they can't) know what he means; he won't be understood by himself either. The illusion of being transparent to one's self is at the heart of logocentrism.[44] If this is Derrida's position, then whether the position is satisfactory depends upon whether his theory about texts, meanings, and interpretations is correct, whether, for example, signs signify only other signs, whether no special weight can be given to any determinate meaning, whether no interpretation can be privileged.

The paradoxes that this Derridean position generates are disturbing, at least to those operating in the tradition of analytic philosophy. That is, if, as the analytic tradition requires, one ought to be rational in discussing theories of interpretation, then interpretation without worry, including the absence of worry Derrida presumably experiences about being understood, would be contingent upon a particular theory being supposed *right* by Derrida and others. But what reason can Derrida and others have for supposing any such thing on Derrida's theory? Doesn't Derrida's theory require the very logocentrism it seeks to undermine?

The preceeding paragraph might elicit the following kinds of response from those operating within the Derridean position. It is assumed in that paragraph that a certain kind of clarity is possible, that by being rational one can obtain a clear understanding of the issues under discussion. But the possibility of such clarity is exactly what Derrida is calling into question. Further, if Derrida does not care about being right, as presumably he does not, then not worrying about being understood in the absence of rightness would not be irrational. The assumption, moreover, that Derrida's position is capable of being right or wrong is itself a questionable one. For Derrideans the question is not whether Derrida's theory is right, but whether there is a need for this theory, and if there is such a need, whether the theory in question fulfills it. Furthermore, not only is Derrida aware that his position requires logocentrism, he is not untroubled by its doing so. In the age of the metaphysics of presence, the concepts available to Derrida to use to undermine that metaphysics are themselves concepts of the metaphysics. Derrida is aware that these concepts have determined his method of reading. But he writes with the conviction that the age of the metaphysics of presence is coming to an end, finding symptoms of this ending in the emergence of, for example, theories like information theory or genetic theory, in which information is encoded in a language which is not the record of speech.[45] When the metaphysics of presence has terminated itself, when 'man and humanism' is transcended, what then? Derrida can 'designate the crevice through which the yet unnameable glimmer beyond the closure (of metaphysics) can be glimpsed'.[46] ('the as yet unnameable which is proclaiming itself and which can do so, as is necessary when ever a birth is in the offing, only under the species of the nonspecies, in the formless, mute, infant, and terrifying form of monstrosity'.[47]

These responses notwithstanding, the fact remains that Derrida must work, before the closure of metaphysics, with the concepts he is trying to call into question. If it were in principle possible to use these concepts to undermine themselves, one could ask why use these concepts in this way? Derrida can't say that undermining is a privilegd way of using these concepts, that it is right to undermine, for nothing is available to justify such a privilege. If, as Derrida believes, the age of metaphysics were coming to an end, then it might be pragmatic to prepare for this end. Whether the phenomena he regards as symptoms of this end are symptoms depends, however, upon Derrida's interpretation of history.

If it were not possible for Derrida to use the concepts of the metaphysics of presence to undermine themselves, then Derrida must step outside those concepts to do the undermining. But before the closure of metaphysics, it is not possible for him to step outside.

It is beyond the scope of this discussion to detail the

difficulties I believe are inherent in what I have represented as Derrida's position (I am aware that a number of quite distinct 'Derridean' positions have issued from the free play of signification opened out by signs in texts bearing Derrida's signature). I shall do instead, if only because I must, what Derrida and his own followers seem to do: decline to act in accordance with a certain major tenet of Derrida's position. In the age of the metaphysics of presence, one cannot but use the concepts of this metaphysics.[58] I shall, therefore, continue to assume that texts have meanings which are privileged by the culture or tradition, and thus that a certain kind of communication is possible, if not always probable, at least among those who share the same form of life. To assume, that is, that customs and habits embedded in forms of life are enough to justify particular interpretations. I am not persuaded, moreover, that Derrida is right in thinking that the age of the metaphysics of presence will come to an end. About the unnameable, I cannot speak.

I shall also continue to assume that we have better or worse understandings of texts – correct and incorrect understandings, not merely more or less ingenious or creative or workable ones – including texts of authors, critics, and metacritics. This may serve as my excuse; it will not, nor is it meant to, serve as adequate justification for so doing from the point of view of those wedded to deconstructionism.

Notes

1 Stanley Fish, 'Interpreting the variorum, *Critical Inquiry* vol. 2 no. 3 (Spring 1976), 474. '[T]he text is taken to be self-sufficient – everything is in it', by those Fish opposes.
2 Ibid., 481. '[I]nterpretive strategies are not put into execution after reading (the pure act of perception in which I do not believe); they are the shape of reading, and because they are the shape of reading, they give texts their shape, making them rather than, as it is usually assumed, arising from them.'
3 Ibid., 483. 'Interpretive communities are made up of those who share interpretive strategies not for reading (in the conventional sense) but for writing texts, for constituting their properties.'
4 At any given time, 'the literary institution' authorizes only a finite number of interpretive strategies. See below.

5 Stanley Fish, 'Normal circumstances, literal language, direct speech acts, the ordinary, the everyday, the obvious, what goes without saying, and other special cases', *Critical Inquiry* vol. 4, no. 4 (Summer 1978), 625–44.

6 Fish argues against defeasibility in interpretive criticism by arguing against what might be called defeasibility$_1$. An interpretation is defeasible$_1$ if it is defeasible in the ways that statements are defeasible or in the ways that hypotheses are defeasible. I shall claim that Fish's argument against defeasibility$_1$ is suspect. Even if his argument were not suspect, what might be called defeasibility$_2$ – an interpretation is defeasible$_2$ if it is defeasible in whatever ways of defeasibility are appropriate for its status – could not be ruled out. That is, even if interpretations had the status Fish assigns to them, they would not in principle be indefeasible: they would in principle be defeasible$_2$. Moreover, since I believe that interpretive remarks do not have the uniform status Fish assigns to them, I believe the defeasibility in interpretive criticism is not limited to the defeasibility that I argue Fish's position must allow.

    While some theorists have assumed that only defeasibility$_1$ is appropriate for interpretive remarks about artworks, I here assume that both defeasibility$_1$ and defeasibility$_2$ are appropriate. If I am correct to assume this (see chapter 8 for my reasons for believing such an assumption can be warranted), then showing that interpretive remarks are indefeasible requires more than showing that they are not defeasible$_1$. It requires showing that they are also not defeasible$_2$. I want to thank Roger Shiner for helpful comments here.

7 Fish, 'Normal circumstances . . .', 627–8.

8 Fish, 'A reply to John Reichert; or, how to stop worrying and learn to love interpretation', *Critical Inquiry* vol. 6, no. 1 (Autumn 1979), 173.

9 Fish, 'Normal circumstances . . .', 627.

10 Ibid., 628.

11 Ibid.

12 Ibid., 629.

13 Ibid.

14 Fish, 'A reply to John Reichert . . .', 173.

15 Fish, 'A reply to John Reichert', *Is There a Text in This Class?* p. 295.The page numbers that follow in parentheses refer to pages in this book.

16 Malcolm Bradbury, 'The state of criticism today', *Contemporary Criticism*, Malcolm Bradbury ed. (New York, 1971), 23.

17 Wollheim, 'A review of Stanley Fish . . .', 65.

18 That is, suppose an interpretation was not defeasible$_1$, defeasible in

just those ways in which statements and hypotheses were defeasible (if 1 were not correct, interpretations would not be defeasible in these ways and hence they would not be defeasible$_1$). However, the interpretation could nevertheless be defeasible$_2$, defeasible in the way appropriate to its status.

19 Wollheim, 'A review of Stanley Fish . . .', 65.

20 Suppose Fish claims that the strategy determines what counts as a change of voice within that strategy. Suppose if condition *a* is met, then one has a change of voice. But whether condition *a* is met or not would itself be independent of the strategy. Does the strategy, for example, determine what it is for a name to appear within that strategy?, does it determine whether Christ's name appears?

21 Does Fish have to say here that when a particular strategy determines whether a character despairs, only that strategy can determine whether a character despairs? Could more than one strategy do that? Suppose that more than one could. Suppose, moreover, as would Fish, that another strategy (or strategies) could determine that despairing were not an option for a character. However, whether one or more than one strategy determines whether a character *can* despair, whether or not a particular character *does* despair is not determined by the strategy alone. For example, in a Marxist strategy there are criteria for the bourgeois exploitation of the proletariat. Whether in a given work such exploitation exists is not determined by the strategy alone. If there were no bourgeois or no proletariat in the work in question, there would be no exploitation of the requisite sort.

22 An interpretation, therefore, can be defeated in the manner of defeat appropriate to its status, it is defeasible$_2$ and hence not indefeasible.

23 Fish, *Is There a Text in This Class?*, p. 346.

24 T. K. Seung, *Structuralism and Hermeneutics* (New York, 1982).

25 M. H. Abrams, 'The deconstructive angel', *Critical Inquiry* vol. 3, no. 3 (Spring 1977), 425–38.

26 All signs on this view are thus independent. 'Independent', can, as Sam Wheeler III has pointed out to me, mean either 'have no connection with' or 'not totally determined by'. The kind of displacement and lack of anchor might then be different under these two readings. In the discussion that follows I do not investigate what possible differences there might be.

27 Jacques Derrida, 'Signature event context', *Glyph*, no. I (1977), 172–97. For independence from individual authors: 181. 'For a writing to be a writing it must continue to "act" and to be readable even when what is called the author of the writing no longer answers for what he has written.' For independence from collective authors or the context of production: 182. 'a written sign carries with it a force

that breaks with its context, that is, with the collectivity of presences organizing the moment of its inscription.' For independence from readers (individual and collective): 179. 'My communication must be repeatable – iterable – in the absolute absence of the receiver or of any empirically determinable collectivity of receivers.' For independence from the objects of signification, the beyond the language referents: 183. 'that absence of the referent and even of the signified meaning, and hence of the correlative intention to signify. If while looking out the window I say: "The sky is blue", this utterance will be intelligible . . . even if the interlocutor does not see the sky; even if I do not see it myself . . .'

28 Cf. Seung, pp. 139–46.

29 Abrams, 'The deconstructive angel', 430.

30 Derrida, 'Signature . . .', 192. 'given that structure of iteration, the intention animating the utterance will never be through and through present to itself and to its content'.

31 Derrida, 'Differance', translated in *Speech and Phenomena and Other Essays on Husserl's Theory of Signs* (Evanston, 1973), 129–61.

32 Abrams, 'The deconstructive angel', 430–1.

33 Stanley Fish, *Is There a Text in This Class?*, p. 268, attempts, 'to dissociate' himself 'from a certain characterization (actually a caricature) of the poststructuralist or Derridian position. In that characterization (represented, for example, by the writings of M. H. Abrams) the denial of objective texts and determinate meanings leads to a universe of absolute free play in which everything is indeterminate and undecidable'. Christopher Norris, *Deconstruction Theory and Practice* (London, 1982), pp. 127–8, claims that: 'Derrida's is not, in other words, a knock-down scepticism easily arrived at and just as easily refuted by a simple *tu quoque* . . . Deconstruction neither denies nor really affects the commonsense view that language exists to communicate meaning. It *suspends* that view for its own specific purpose of seeing what happens when the writs of convention no longer run.'

34 Jacques Derrida, 'Living On', *Deconstruction and Criticism*, Harold Bloom et al, eds (London, 1979), 84.

35 William Tolhurst, 'On what a text is and how it means', *British journal of Aesthetics* no. 19 (1979), 3–14. Tolhurst distinguishes among sentence meaning, utterer's meaning, and utterance meaning.

36 It is not a 'hermeneutic deciphering, the decoding of a meaning or truth', 'Signature . . .', 195.

37 Jacques Derrida, 'La structure, le signe et le jeu dans le discours des sciences humaines', in *L'Écriture et la différence* (Paris, 1967), 427,

cited in Abrams, 431.

38 Cf. Mark Taylor, 'Deconstruction: what's the difference?' *National Humanities Center Newsletter*, vol. 5, no. 1 (Fall 1983), 24–9.

39 Jacques Derrida, 'Restitutions of truth to size, de la vérité en peinture', translated by John P. Leavey, Jr, pp. 1–42.

40 I am interested in what is going on 'philosophically'. As Steven Melville pointed out to me, Derrida may have many aims. Some of these aims I would not call philosophical. That is, Derrida may want 'to display the ways in which Schapiro and Heidegger are laced together by the shoes or the painting of them, the ways in which the pair they make is a version of the pair the painting makes . . .'.

41 Derrida, 'Restitutions', p. 42.

42 '[T]he original or transcendental signified, is never absolutely present outside a system of differences. The absence of the transcendental signified extends the domain of the interplay of signification infinitely.' Jacques Derrida, 'Structure, sign, and play in the discourse of the human sciences', *Writing and Difference*, 280.

43 Derrideans might claim that while it is not 'right' to view Schapiro in this way, it is therapeutic and freeing to do so, for by doing so we can see what our fundamental commitments are. But to see what our commitments are is not to see why these commitments should be given up.

44 In this discussion I have contrasted privileged determinate meaning with free play and based understanding on the former. I have not discussed whether there are other alternatives and whether, therefore, Derrida's attack against 'understanding oneself' and 'being understood by others' would stand against these when alternatively understood.

45 I want to thank Mary Wiseman for her generous attempts to make my reading of Derrida less of a caricature. Her remarks about the charting a Derridean interpreter has to do, the absence of any privilege for an intepretation, the possibility of an unworkable interpretation, the awareness on Derrida's part of his own dependence on logocentrism and his belief in the end of the age of the metaphysics of presence were particularly helpful. I do not wish, however, to imply that she would agree with the positions I take on these views.

46 Jacques Derrida, *Of Grammatology* (Baltimore, 1977), p. 14.

47 Jacques Derrida, *Writing and Difference* (London, 1978), p. 293.

48 Like Clov in Beckett's *Endgame* we use the words that we have been taught. If they don't mean anything anymore, we need to be taught others. Or we must remain silent.

7

Status and Acceptability Standard: Kinds of Defeasibility

If, as I have argued in chapters 4 through 6, the status of statement is not a priori ruled out for interpretive remarks – if it is in principle possible that some interpretive remarks are statements – this would not preclude the possibility that others are hypotheses, or reports of experiences-as, or prescriptions. Nor would it preclude indefinitely many other possibilities, e.g., the possibility that yet other interpretive remarks are judgements or characterizing remarks, or some combination of statement and prescription, or of prescription and report, and so on. In this chapter I focus primarily on the four canonical statuses previously mentioned – statements, hypotheses, reports of experiences-as, and prescriptions. First I detail the kinds of defeasibility that would be appropriate to interpretive remarks if interpretive remarks had any of these statuses. I take particular care in spelling out the kinds of defeasibility that are possible here for I want to show conclusively that only one kind of status allows for defeat by a relevant counterpossibility. I then turn to critical practice to see what it reveals about the presence of these statuses and kinds of defeasibility. If, as I believe, defeat by a relevant counterpossibility is a typical mode of defeat in criticism, then one has sufficient reason for regarding many of the interpretive remarks critics make as statements.

Kinds of defeasibility

In uttering (let 'uttering' refer to either speaking or writing) 'Poe's subjects are unmotivated treachery and self-violence', a critic may be interpreting. If, in interpreting, a critic were, for example, stating that Poe's subjects are unmotivated treachery and self-violence, then he might also be knowledge-claiming, that is, he might be claiming to know that it was true that these are Poe's subjects.

Critics who interpret frequently claim to know: consider, for example, the critic who claimed to know that the altar-pieces depicting a woman carrying a platter of severed breasts were representations of St Agnes, or the critic to whom it was obvious (and if obvious, then known$_k$) that the satyr represented the powers of darkness. If, in cases like these (and cases like these are frequent in criticism), the critic were knowledge-claiming, that is, he was claiming to know that it was true that x is F, then, I argue, we could explain why criticism tolerates multiple, sometimes even contrary, interpretations of artworks without having to give up certain other initially plausible beliefs about criticism and artworks. That is, we would not have (1) to deny that direct critical confrontation and significant defeat regularly take place between critics, whether the critics use similar of different conceptual frameworks or methodologies. We would also not have either (2) to require that artworks have a special ontic status or (3) to require that all interpretive remarks be other than statements and have an acceptability standard other than truth and falsity. Explanations of critical tolerance have traditionally had to do (1), (2), or (3), or some combination of (1), (2), and (3).

In chapter 4 I argued that criticism could tolerate incompatible interpretations, if, for example, these interpretations satisfied conflicting criteria and we had no reason for choosing one criterion over the other. No mention was made of critical challenge and defeat; both interpretations were acceptable. In this chapter, I discuss a kind of critical challenge and defeat that I argue is compatible with critical tolerance.

If, in interpreting, a critic were *hypothesizing* that Poe's subjects are unmotivated treachery and self-violence, then he might be – as I shall call it – '*plausibility-claiming*'; that is, he might be claiming to know that it was plausible that these are Poe's subjects.[1] I shall perhaps somewhat misleadingly call the claim made here a plausibility claim. Although what I call a plausibility claim is a knowledge claim, I call it such in order to emphasize its difference from other knowledge claims, in particular, from claims to know that it is true that x is F. In a plausibility claim what is claimed to be known is not the truth of one's classifications (not that it is true that x is F) but their plausibility (that is is plausible that x is F). I shall consider the kinds of defeasibility that would be available in interpretive criticism if critics, in interpreting, were either knowledge-claiming, plausibility-claiming, reporting an experience-as or prescribing.

I am (for the moment) leaving open the possibility that a given utterance of the words 'Poe's subjects are unmotivated treachery and self-violence' may be both an interpretive remark and a knowledge claim, or be both an interpretive remark and a plausibility claim. One might suppose that to defeat the knowledge claim, in such a case, is to defeat the interpretive remark, but it is a mistake to suppose this. One defeats an utterance under some description; it is a mistake, therefore, to think that to defeat the utterance *qua* knowledge claim or *qua* plausibility claim is to defeat it *qua* interpretive remark. If a critic interprets Poe's subjects as unmotivated treachery and self-violence, his interpretation is not shown to be false, or implausible, or otherwise unsuccessful by the defeat of his claim to know that it is true, or to know that it is plausible, that these are Poe's subjects.

For cases where a critical utterance is both an interpretive remark and a knowledge claim, I concentrate on the defeasibility of the knowledge claim; where a critical utterance is both an interpretive remark and a plausibility claim, I concentrate on the defeasibility of the plausibility claim (recall that I am leaving open the possibility that there may be such cases). Later in the discussion I try to show that there are in fact such cases and that in these cases the critical challenge most frequently is directed against the utterance *qua* knowledge or plausibility claim rather than against the utterance *qua* interpretive remark.[2] It is for this reason that I concentrate in these cases on the defeasibility of the knowledge or plausibility claim.

The possibilities of defeating a critic's knowledge claim

If a critic, in uttering 'Poe's subjects are unmotivated treachery and self-violence' ('x is F'), is both stating and knowledge-claiming – i.e., claiming to know that it is true that Poe's subjects are unmotivated treachery and self-violence – the critic's knowledge claim is subject to defeat in the following ways:[3]

(1) If one could show it to be false that x is F, then the critic could not be said to know that it is true that x is F.

(2) One could also defeat the critic's claim to know that it was true that x is F, if one could show that the critic was not justified in believing it to be true that x is F, whether or not it was true that x is F, either by showing that

(a) the critic lacked the requisite ability to recognize that it was true that x is F, or if, given that he had the ability in general, on the particular occasion in question his ability was impaired – he was inattentive, careless, drugged, or the like; or by showing that

(b) the critic has not ruled out a relevant counter-possibility. 'P' expresses a relevant counter-possibility to that expressed by 'it is true that x is F, if and only if

(i) it is not logically possible for 'it is true that x is F' and 'p' jointly to be true, and

(ii) the critic has adequate warrant for thinking that it is true that x is F only if he has adequate warrant for thinking that 'p' is false.[4]

This last sort of defeat is, I argue, the more important sort of defeat for interpretive remarks in art criticism. For an example of this kind of defeat consider Henry James's *The Turn of the Screw*. Let 'p' be 'it is true that *The Turn of the Screw* is a study in the hallucinatory effects of repressed sexuality'; let 'it is true that x is F' be 'it is true that *The Turn of the Screw* is a ghost story'. If a critic would not be justified in claiming to know that it is true that *The Turn of the Screw* is a ghost story without possessing adequate warrant for thinking it false that it is a study in the hallucinatory effects of repressed sexuality and if it were not logically possible for 'it is true that *The Turn of the Screw* is a ghost story' and 'it is true that *The Turn of the Screw* is a study in the hallucinatory effects of repressed sexuality' jointly to be true (assume that whatever ghosts are, they are not hallucinations), then 'it is true that *The Turn of the Screw* is a study in the hallucinatory effects of repressed sexuality' would express a relevant counterpossibility to what is expressed by the claim 'it is true that *The Turn of the Screw* is a ghost story'. The critic's failure to have ruled out this relevant counterpossibility would defeat the critic's claim to know that *The Turn of the Screw* is a ghost story.

The possibilities of defeating a critic's plausibility claim

If a critic, in uttering 'Poe's subjects are unmotivated treachery and self-violence' ('*x* is *F*'), is hypothesizing and plausibility-claiming – i.e., claiming to know that it is plausible that Poe's subjects are unmotivated treachery and self-violence – then the critic's plausibility claim could be defeated in ways analogous to some of those just discussed.

If one could show that the critic was in the first way mentioned above not justified in believing it to be plausible that *x* is *F* – the critic lacked the requisite ability to recognize that it is plausible that *x* is *F*, or given that he had the ability in general, on the particular occasion in question his ability was impaired – then the critic's claim to know that it is plausible that *x* is *F* would be defeated. Notice that I am not claiming that showing that the critic did not have the ability to recognize that it is plausible that *x* is *F*, or that this ability to recognize was impaired, would by itself show that the claim that *x* is *F* was itself implausible or indefensible or unreasonable. What I am claiming is that it would show that the critic's claim to know that it was plausible that *x* is *F* was defeated.

Let us see whether the second way of showing that the critic was not justified in believing that *x* is *F* – pointing to a relevant counterpossibility that the critic has not ruled out – is available when the believing in question is not believing that it is true that *x* is *F* (as it was in the earlier case) but is believing that it is plausible that *x* is *F*. We are interested here in whether a critic's claim to know that it is plausible that *x* is *F* can be defeated by showing that the critic was not justified in believing that it is plausible that *x* is *F* because he has not ruled out a relevant counterpossibility.

'*P*' expresses a relevant counterpossibility to that expressed by 'it is plausible that *x* is *F*' if and only if (i) it is not logically possible for 'it is plausible that *x* is *F*' and '*p*' jointly to be true, and (ii) the critic has adequate warrant for thinking that it is plausible that *x* is *F* only if he has adequate warrant for thinking that '*p*' is false.

Let us see what happens in *The Turn of the Screw* case if the critic, instead of knowledge-claiming, were plausibility-claiming. 'It is plausible that *The Turn of the Screw* is a study in the hallucinatory effects of repressed sexuality' ('*p*') expresses a relevant counterpossibility to what is expressed by the claim 'it is plausible that *The Turn of the Screw* is a ghost story' ('*x* is *F*') only if conditions (i) and (ii) are met. But any claim of the form 'it is plausible that *x* is *G*' – 'it is plausible that *The Turn of the Screw* is a study in the hallucinatory effects of repressed sexuality' is of this form – cannot satisfy condition (i).

When I speak in condition (i) of it not being logically possible for 'it is plausible that *x* is *F*' and '*p*' *jointly to be true*. I mean that with respect to these two sentences and no others, *each* is true. I do not mean by 'jointly to be true' that the sentence formed by the operator 'it is plausible that' and the conjunction of the two embedded sentences is true.

There is, however, one candidate for '*p*' that does satisfy condition (i). If '*p*' is 'it is *not in any way plausible* that *x* is *F*', then it is not logically possible for it to be true that 'it is plausible that *x* is *F*' and for it also to be true that 'it is not in any way plausible that *x* is *F*'.

Whether this candidate for '*p*' also satisfies condition (ii) is not an easy matter to settle, for whether the condition is satisfied is conditional upon knowing the truth about epistemic justification. Since it is not clear what the truth about this is, it is not clear whether condition (ii) is satisfied. Let us suppose, however, that the condition were satisfied. That is, let us suppose that a critic would not have adequate warrant for thinking it to be plausible that *x* is *F* unless he had adequate warrant for thinking 'it is not in any way plausible that x is F is false, then 'it is not in any way plausible that x is F' would express a relevant counterpossibility to what is expressed by the claim 'it is plausible that x is F'.

If we look at critical practice, however, we shall see that critics do not attempt to defeat a critic's claim that it is plausible that x is F by showing that it is *in no way* plausible that x is F. Critics do not characteristically regard their fellow critics as complete fools, that is, the parties in a significant critical debate do not regard their opponent as offering an interpretation that is *in no way* plausible. While a critic may try to show that it is implausible that x is F or that it is false that x is F, to show either of these things, is not to show that it is no way plausible that x is F.

What critics most frequently do in interpretive disputes is to provide an alternative to 'x *is* F' of the form 'x is G'. Whatever we finally decide critics are doing when they provide this alternative, one candidate for what they are doing – viz., showing that it is in no way plausible that x is F – appears to be unsatisfactory.

For the purposes of our discussion, therefore, defeat of a critic's plausibility claim, the defeat of his claim to know that it is plausible that x is F, cannot be accomplished by pointing to a relevant counterpossibility that the critic has not ruled out. The only candidate for a relevant counterpossibility that has a chance of satisfying conditions (i) and (ii) – 'it is in no way plausible that x is F' – is unsatisfactory for the reason previously given.

Showing it to be false that x is F would not defeat the critic's claim to know that it was plausible that x is F. A critic can be justified in claiming to know that it is plausible that x is F even when he knows it to be false that x is F; 'having a show of truth or reasonableness', as 'plausible' is understood, is consistent with being false. For example, a person may be justified in claiming to know a story to be plausible despite the fact that he knows the story to be false.

The possibilities of defeating a critic's report of an experience-as

If a critic, in uttering 'Poe's subjects are unmotivated treachery and self-violence', is reporting an experience-as, i.e., is reporting seeing or hearing x as F, and if hearing or seeing x as F is necessary for understanding x as F ('understanding', we saw in chapter 3 is not to be identified with the 'knowing that' that entails justified true belief), then the critic's interpretive remark could also be defeated in some ways analogous to those mentioned above.

That is, if one could show that a critic did not have the general ability to have experiences of the appropriate sort, that he did not have the requisite recognized background of behavior, then he could not be said to see or hear x as F and hence could not be said to understand x as F. Moreover, if one could show that although the critic had the general ability to have the appropriate kind of experience, his ability was impaired on the specific occasion in question – he was inattentive, or careless, he wasn't aware of significant properties of the object – then the critic's claim to see or hear x as F could be defeated.

This sort of defeat is not as important a defeat as would be the defeat by a relevant counterpossibility. However, if the critic both had the requisite unimpaired ability and claimed to see or hear x as F, then there would be no further way to defeat this claim to understand x as F. An analogue to a relevant counterpossibility is not available.[5] 'P' would express a 'relevant counterpossibility' to what is expressed by 'I experience x as F' if and only if (i) it is not logically possible for 'I experience x as F' and 'p' jointly to be true and (ii) the critic has adequate warrant for believing himself to experience x as F only if he has adequate warrant for believing that 'p' is false.

However, it is logically possible for '*The Turn of the Screw* is experienced as a study in the hallucinatory effects of repressed sexuality' ('p') and 'I experience *The Turn of the Screw* as a ghost story' ('I experience x as F') jointly to be true. Condition (i) for an analogue to a relevant counterpossibility is not satisfied.

Showing that x is F is false would not defeat the critic's claim to have experienced x as F, for the critic is not claiming that x has the property F, but only that x have the aspect F. Although a report of an experience-as can be true or false – the person has or does not have the experience – the experience reported is neither true nor false.

It would, however, be possible for one critic's experience of x

as F to be more successful than another critic's experience of x as G, where by 'successful' is meant that more people were able also to have the experience of hearing or seeing x as F than were able to have the experience of hearing or seeing x as G. But the success of 'x as F' in this sense would not undermine the critic's claim to have experienced x as G nor his claim to understand x as G, assuming both critics are equally competent and knowledgeable. Success or lack of it is independent of understanding. If no one were able to experience x as G, one might suspect some eccentricity in the critic, for one accepts or rejects a critic's claims on the basis of one's own hearing or seeing-as experiences. However, it would be possible simply to acknowledge diversity.

The possibilities of defeating a critic's prescription

If a critic, in uttering 'Poe's subjects are unmotivated treachery and self-violence', is prescribing that Poe's subjects should be viewed as unmotivated treachery and self-violence, then the critic's prescription could be defeated in the following ways.

If one could show that one could not obey the prescription, then one would have defeated the prescription. I am relying here on the commonly accepted belief that 'ought' implies 'can'. For example, the prescription: 'View Nora (in Ibsen's play *A Doll's House*) as simultaneously leaving her home entirely unhappy, with noone to live for, and as entirely happy and independent', would be defeated since it cannot be obeyed: it is not possible for a critic to view her in both ways simultaneously.

Prescriptions of the kind said to be found in art criticism presuppose standards – 'F is a way to view x if one wants to be a proper or a discriminating or an informed or a sensitive viewer'. Insofar as a prescription requires a standard of this sort, if it could be shown that a viewer who satisfied the requisite standard would not regard x as F – suppose, for example, that regarding x as F required one to disregard or contradict what seemed to be significant properties of the work, and no good reason for disregarding or contradicting these was provided – then one would have grounds for ruling out such a prescription.[6]

An analogue of defeating a knowledge claim, 'x is F', by showing that a relevant counterpossibility, 'p', has not been ruled out, is not available for prescriptions. '*P*' would express a 'relevant counterpossibility' to what is expressed by 'Regard *x* as *F*' if and only if (i) it is not logically possible for 'Regard *x* as *F*' and '*p*' jointly to be obeyed and (ii) the critic has adequate warrant for regarding *x* as *F* only if he has adequate warrant for not doing '*p*'. In this case the adequate warrant referred to is not epistemic warrant. What then is adequate warrant here? In order to answer this question we would have to know what sound practical reasoning is. Given this difference in warrant, moreover, one could question whether we have anything here we should call a 'relevant counterpossibility', even if we are careful to keep these terms in quotes. Fortunately, we do not have to decide these questions for whatever is specified by these conditions is not available.

Let '*p*' be 'Regard Pamela (in Richardson's novel of that name) as a crafty, hypocritical girl'; let 'Regard *x* as *F*' be 'Regard Pamela as a virtuous virgin'.[7] Let us assume that being a virtuous virgin does not allow for any hypocrisy[8] and that one competent critic regards her as a virtuous virgin and that another equally competent critic regards her as a crafty, hypocritical girl. In these circumstances it is logically possible for the two prescriptions to be jointly obeyed.[9] Condition (i) for an analogue to a relevant counterpossibility is not satisfied.

Showing that *x* is *F* is false would not defeat the critic's prescription to regard *x* as *F*, for the critic is not claiming that *x* has the property *F*. Prescriptions are neither true nor false.

If what I have said about kinds of defeasibility is correct, then only in cases where interpretive statements are knowledge claims can one defeat the knowledge claim by showing that the critic has not ruled out a relevant counterpossibility. Relevant counterpossibilities are not available in art criticism for defeating either plausibility claims, reports of an experience-as or prescriptions. On any of these four canonical statuses, however, there is room for debate, for example, debate about competency, or about the adequacy of one's knowledge of the object's properties. All thus leave room for defeat of one sort or another, e.g., a critic's remark is not known to be true or is not known to be plausible, the interpretive remark is not a report or a genuine seeing- or hearing-as experience, it is a recommendation that either cannot be carried out or its carrying out requires unjustified distortions.

A look at critical practice

Some sample critical controversies

If we look at critical practice, we find critics challenging one another's interpretive remarks in any number of ways. I shall examine a few instances of such practice in order to determine whether they provide support for one rather than another status and acceptability standard, for one rather than another kind of defeasibility.

For example, consider a controversy centered around the following lines from Milton's Paradise Lost:

>   then let those
> Contrive who need, or when they need, not now,
> For while they sit contriving, shall the rest
> Millions that stand in arms, and longing wait
> The signal to ascend, sit ling'ring here
> Heav'ns fugitives . . . [10]

Some critics claim to have found a contradiction in these lines as 'Millions that stand in arms could not at the same time sit ling'ring'.[11] However, as one critic has pointed out, while it is true that millions could not both stand and sit simultaneously, 'Milton doesn't say they could. He has a future and a present tense:

>   *Shall* the rest
> Millions that stand in arms, and longing wait
> The signal to ascend, sit ling'ring here.'[12]

The latter critic is trying to show that the critical claim – 'there is a contradiction in these lines of Milton' – is false. If it is false, it follows that any critic who claims that there is such a contradiction is mistaken. I think it is clear that this kind of controversy would lose its point if the claimants did not understand one another to be making statements. Moreover, since this controversy is essentially a grammatical one, about what the verb tenses are, and about what the logical implications of verbs in certain tenses are, and not about what the work's *aspects* are, or what properties may be *imputed* to the work, or in what ways the work *should be regarded*,[13] any of the four canonical views about the status of interpretations could regard the claim – 'there is a contradiction in these lines of Milton' – as a non-interpretive claim, and thus as an ordinary statement purporting to express knowledge.

Suppose, however, that a critic uses the alleged contradiction as part of his support for a more general claim: 'In *Paradise Lost*, the music of Milton's rhetoric disguises its lack of sense.'[14] This critic's claim is not shown to be mistaken by showing that one set of lines, alleged not to have sense, does have sense. Let us imagine, moreover, that in the other examples the critic uses to support his general claim, the question of whether the lines have sense or not is not easily settled. That is, one cannot show without question that they do or do not have sense.

In this case we cannot show that it is false that, or it is in no way plausible that, the lines lack sense and hence that it is false that, or in no way plausible that, Milton's rhetoric disguises its lack of sense. We also cannot show that a recommendation to regard Milton's rhetoric as disguising the lack of sense cannot be obeyed or to obey it requires unjustified distortion; or that an experience of Milton's rhetoric as disguising the lack of sense could not be a genuine experience-as. I suggest, moreover, that in typical significant critical controversies these things cannot be shown. In this kind of case, is any critical challenge and defeat possible?

If in this case it could be shown that the critic had not ruled out a relevant counterpossibility, then defeat would be possible. However, if such defeat were possible then this is already to presuppose something about the nature of the claim; defeat of a claim by showing that a relevant counterpossibility has not been ruled out is possible in art criticism only for claims to know.

If a critic in interpreting is knowledge-claiming, then his interpretation has to be meant as a statement which is true or false. I shall argue that critical practice suggests that critics are frequently knowledge-claiming and, therefore, that their interpretations are meant as statements. It shall also, I hope become clear that the defeat of a knowledge claim by showing that a relevant counterpossibility has not been ruled out is a common occurrence in interpretive criticism in the arts.

Statements and defeat by a relevant counterpossibility

While it is clear that critics frequently take themselves to be knowledge-claiming – one philosopher has suggested that a 'critical position will finally rest upon calling a claim *obvious*'[15] – as we saw earlier a question has been raised about whether critics are misguided about the nature of their own activity. Might a critic who says 'the tiger is unambiguously and obviously evil' be plausibility-claiming, or reporting an experience-as or prescribing?

I see no good reason for believing that critics are misguided when they take themselves to be knowledge-claiming. I have already dealt with some of the reasons given for this alleged critical misguidance. I contend that critics not only frequently do make knowledge claims, either explicitly, 'I know that . . .', or implicitly, 'There is no doubt that . . .', critics also frequently challenge one another's knowledge claims by trying to show that relevant counterpossibilities have not been ruled out.

For example, there is, I maintain, good reason for regarding the critic who says '[t]here can be no doubt that 'The Tyger' is a poem that celebrates the holiness of tigerness'[16] as providing a relevant counterpossibility that has not been ruled out by the critic who claims to know that 'The Tyger' is about the evilness of tigerness (assume that whatever holiness is, it is not evil). If we view a substantial amount of what goes on in art criticism in this way, then we can explain why artworks tolerate multiple, even contrary, interpretations without having to deny what seems to many to be an obvious characteristic of such practice, namely, that critics in cases like the one described above do directly challenge and defeat one another. If the one critic were claiming to know that it was plausible that 'The Tyger' is about the evilness of tigerness, this would not directly challenge the other critic who was claiming to know that it was plausible that 'The Tyger' is about the holiness of tigerness (assume here that both interpretations have roughly the same textual support and are conformable to admissible myths). Nor would the experiencing of the tiger as holy challenge the experiencing of the tiger as evil, if both experiencers were equally competent as experiencers. The prescriptions: 'View the tiger as evil', and 'View the tiger as holy', might both provide a proper or an interesting way of viewing the tiger. If, however, the critic is taken in this case to be claiming that she knows that the tiger is evil, then if 'the tiger is holy' is a relevant counterpossibility that she has not ruled out, her claim to know it to be true that the tiger is evil will have been defeated. This way of viewing the case has a further advantage: critical interpretations can be, although not all of them need be, statements.

What has not been clearly understood in these cases, however, is the nature of the critical challenge and defeat. While showing that a critic has not ruled out a relevant counterpossibility directly challenges the critic's claim to know, this challenge is compatible with the legitimate presence in criticism of multiple, even incompatible interpretations, since even if successful, it only defeats the critic's claim to know, it does not defeat the claim *qua* interpretive claim. Critics, I believe, frequently overestimate the effects of challenges of this kind, for they assume that the relevant counterpossibility they provide has shown the original interpretation to be false, when it has not.

For example, consider Edmund Wilson's suggestion: '*The Turn of the Screw* is a study in the hallucinatory effects of repressed sexuality'. Even if this has not been ruled out as a possible way of viewing the story, that fact would not show that the interpretive claim made by another critic, '*The Turn of the Screw* is a ghost story', is false, but only that the critic who claimed that the story was a ghost story could not claim to know this. Alternatively, if viewing *The Turn of the Screw* as a ghost story has not been ruled out as a possible way of viewing it, then this would show, not that Wilson's interpretive claim is false, but only that he cannot claim to know that *The Turn of the Screw* is a study of the kind in question.

Or suppose, as Roger Scruton suggests, there are two ways of hearing a certain passage from Beethoven's *Diabelli Variations* because there are two distinct ways of grouping the sound sequences.[17] Moreover, suppose that one critic hears the passage's ending as tense, and another critic hears it as relaxed. If neither critic can rule out the other's claim, then neither critic could claim to know that the ending is the way he states it to be, although the relevant counterpossibility provided by the other's claim would not show that either interpretation is false.

It does not follow, of course, from the fact that many knowledge claims are defeated, that all will be defeated. In chapter 4, in the blaze of light example, I suggested (in effect) that limits might be set upon what could count as a relevant counterpossibility, thereby disqualifying Buddhist or atheistic interpretations, for example, as relevant counterpossibilities to the Catholic interpretation.

If I am correct, defeat by a relevant counterpossibility of a critic's explicit or implicit claim to know is a common mode of defeat in the critical realm. I want now to suggest why, with regard to certain kinds of interpretive remarks, it may always be available as a mode of defeat.

There is, I believe, some reason to suppose that a special kind of precision is required of certain interpretive claims in art criticism, in particular of those claims which attempt to say what a work expresses. (The interpretive claims in question here are statements purporting to express knowledge.) This precision is required of these claims in the sense that an interpretive remark about what a work expresses is known to be true only if it satisfies the precision requirement. Interestingly, a consequence of this requirement turns out to be that it is conceptually impossible, and not merely practically impossible, to establish such an interpretive remark as true. I shall try now to spell this out more fully, and to show that the conceptual impossibility in question is due to the fact that relevant counterpossibilities could not be ruled out.

Critics frequently make claims about what artworks express; they make claims about what the work as a whole expresses ('the poem is dignified') and they make claims about what parts of it express ('Lear is sarcastic when he says – "on my knees I beg that you'll vouchsafe me raiment, bed, and food".') If, in order to be known to be true, such claims were required to be known to be precisely right, that is, known to be right to the extent that no further significant distinction could be made with regard to them, then it would be conceptually impossible to establish these claims as true.

Whether the demand for precision that operates in connection with critical claims of the indicated sort is a demand for a statement which is known to be precisely right, a demand for what can be called 'absolute precision', is not an easy matter to settle. While a cursory look at critical practice reveals that precision matters – critics frequently praise the finely tuned sensibilities of their colleagues – they engage in debates about whether a critical remark which seems precisely right to one of them is not in fact slightly or even grossly off[18] – it is not clear to me that any individual critic does demand a statement known to be precisely right. It seems more reasonable to suppose that the critical enterprise *as a whole* has as an epistemic aim – i.e., as an aim partly definitive, by way of a necessary condition, of such epistemic success, such *knowledge*, as it strives to achieve – not stopping short of such precision. The coherence of critical practice, for example, would be explainable in terms of the practice's demand for absolute precision for this demand would make coherent the critics use of, and attempt to improve upon, previous critical claims. While the demand for absolute precision is not the only way to make coherent critics' attempts to improve upon previous claims, the demand – always try to be more precise than before – could do so as well, it seems not unreasonable to suppose that a desire for ever more precision is fuelled by a desire to be precisely right. If the enterprises did indeed have the aim of absolute precision, then, since in criticism (1) there is no limit to the number of distinctions that can be made, and (2) there is no non-arbitrary way of ruling out the possibility of a further distinction being significant, there would be no way of telling that any individual critic's statement was precisely right.

Requiring a statement to be precisely right generates a difficulty when conditions (1) and (2) are satisfied. When these conditions are not satisfied, finding the precisely right statement can be quite simple. If one were asked, for example, how many books one bought on Tuesday, how many people attended one's lecture, or what the length of one's desk (rounding off to the nearest inch) was, one would ordinarily have no difficulty determining the precisely right answers. Even if one were asked in the desk case to give the desk's length in terms of fractions of an inch up to five decimal places, the precisely right answer would in principle be available. One might have more difficulty finding it given that the demand for increased precision would require finer discriminations, but the difficulty here would be practical, not conceptual.

The situation changes, however, when one is required to give the *exact* length of the desk, i.e., no rounding off to the nearest decimal place allowed. In this case one could not, however precise one's measuring instrument, come up with an answer that one would be entitled to claim was the precisely right one. Whatever answer one's measuring instrument gave, there would always be an unlimited number of answers, all compatible with this one, such that one could not rule out the desk's compliance with any of them.

For example, suppose that one's measuring instrument's capacity were five decimal places, and that one had determined that the desk was seven feet 3.00000 inches long. There would be an unlimited number of other measurements – seven feet 3.000001, seven feet 3.0000001, seven feet 3.000000 . . .1 inches and so on – with which the desk could comply. If one's measuring instrument's capacity achieved six decimal places, one could rule out some of these, but there would always be an unlimited number one could not rule out. This is the case *whatever the level of precision.*[19]

If, on the other hand, limits are set establishing what counts as a significant difference in length – if, for example, any distinction beyond the hundredth decimal place is taken to be insignificant – then one could in principle (and if one's instruments were fine enough, one could in practice) determine the precisely right answer. In order to respond to Vladimir's 'This is becoming really insignificant' with Estragon's 'Not enough', one must establish what differences do, and what differences do not, make a significant difference.

Precision in criticism is, of course, not understood in terms of measuring quantities. However, measurement is not the only area in which it makes sense to ask for precision. In criticism, as in other domains, precision is bound up with making distinctions. In discussing works, critics make choices about, for example, which classifications to use with a work, which comparisons to make, which features to emphasize. Questions of precision can arise with regard to any of these choices.

Given that in a natural language general classifications include more specific ones – 'thing' includes 'living thing' and 'blackbird' – going from more general classifications to more specific classifications is frequently a move toward increased precision. For example, if we agree that Lear says 'on my knees I beg that you'll vouchsafe me raiment, bed, and food' sarcastically rather than genuinely beseechingly, then asking what admixture, if there is an admixture, of demand or scorn or bathos or appeal or bargaining or warning pervades his sarcasm is an attempt at further precision.

It remains to be shown, however, that in criticism the two conditions I mentioned earlier do in fact hold. If they do, and if a critical statement about expression were required to be known to be precisely right, then one could never know that any such statement was precisely right.

In determining what a work expresses, critics use a natural language, a language which provides for an unlimited number of characters – words singly or in combination. The critic's task is to decide which critical words fit a particular work. Consider, for example, a literary critic confronting Hamm's words 'forgive me' in Beckett's *Endgame*. 'Forgive me' means something different depending on whether it is said sincerely, or bitterly, or ironically, or hollowly, or mirthlessly, or mockingly, or with hollow bitterness, or ironical bitterness, or between irony and mockery and so on. Beckett's stage directions indicate that Hamm says it 'coldly', but there are mocking, hollow, ironical and so on coldnesses.

An unlimited number of phrases are available which might appropriately describe Hamm's utterance. This is the case even if one also knows that Hamm's insistent use of the terms 'forgive me' occurs in a context unaccommodating to it. If boundaries are not set as to what counts as a significant difference in discrimination, then, no matter how finely tuned one's critical sensibilities were, it would at any point be conceptually impossible to rule out the utterance's compliance with a number of phrases. If, for example, between ironic forgiveness and mocking forgiveness there is that forgiveness which we can describe as 'the forgiveness between ironic and mocking forgiveness', and between this latter forgiveness and ironic forgiveness there is that forgiveness which we can describe as 'the forgiveness between ironic forgiveness and the forgiveness between ironic and mocking forgiveness', and so on, then unless it is indicated when further discrimination is insignificant, it would be impossible in principle to determine with which of the indefinite plurality of such descriptions a given utterance complies.[20]

Although we have the means for describing different forgivenesses *ad infinitum*,[21] might it not be claimed that nature has done the work of setting up limits, of establishing what counts as significant difference? One might wish to claim that there wasn't any forgiveness between the forgiveness between ironic forgiveness and mocking forgiveness and ironic forgiveness. It could be argued that there are boundaries that nature has set, and when one runs up against these one has come to the end of one's inquiry. One can determine either that the forgiveness in question is the one between ironic forgiveness and mocking forgiveness, or else that it is ironic forgiveness. Although it might be difficult to determine which of these it is (the difference between them may be subtle), it would be in principle possible to finish; there could be complete warrant for asserting that it is the one and not the other of them.

The contention here is, in effect, that even if condition (1) obtained in that there was in theory no limit to the number of distinctions that could be made, condition (2) does not obtain, for there is a non-arbitrary way of ruling out the possibility of further significant distinction. Since the joint satisfaction of these conditions was sufficient for the impossibility in question, what is claimed here is that one argument for such impossibility won't work.

We do not need to address directly the issue of whether or not there is a limit in nature to the kinds of forgiveness possible, for, even if there were such a limit, it is not reasonable to suppose that one had reached it. Authors have shown, and as far as we can tell will continue to show, that there are more kinds of forgiveness than one had thought possible. It seems conceivable that an author could provide a context in which one felt obliged to say that the forgiveness was neither the one between ironic forgiveness and mocking forgiveness, or ironic forgiveness, but some forgiveness between these two. Just as we may learn from microtonal music to discriminate more tones, or from impressionist paintings more shades of color, so too from literary works we may learn to discriminate forgivenesses. I see no reason to suppose of any particular compliance class of forgiveness provided for in the language that it has to be empty. That we do not find it important in our ordinary dealings to separate compliance classes of forgiveness does not foreclose the possibility that we could learn to distinguish among such classes and to regard such distinctions as important.

If it is not clear what limits there are in nature, then, if there are limits in critical inquiry, the critics must set them. Critics who try to convince their readers that further discrimination would be insignificant enough – the poem is dignified, Lear is sarcastic – certainly act as if there were limits. But can we be certain that the limits are where a given critic says they are? Although some critics may urge us to stop with their level of discernment, the history of criticism suggests, perhaps even overwhelming suggests, that no *general* answer as to what counts as the maximum fineness of discrimination could be claimed to be satisfactory: countless works thought precisely understood by one generation or group of critics have in the hands of another been more subtly perceived. One critic's subtle perceptions have led to previously unimaginable further subtleties. Moreover, what is considered subtle at one time may be regarded as grossly inaccurate at another, or vice versa. It is unlikely to be possible definitely to establish when further discrimination is irrelevant, if what counts as relevant discrimination itself undergoes alteration.

What is shown in a work depends upon groupings critics select for the work. Given that different critics have different interests and purposes, they will sort works into different groups and the properties that are taken to be exemplified and expressed will vary. This is not to deny that certain groupings are more characteristic than others. Artworks are regularly sorted, for example, into tragedies, comedies, romances; they are described as Gothic, Baroque, and so on. But regroupings are always possible. Some – like labeling *King Lear* and *Endgame* 'comedies' – determine not only which features of the plays one takes to be significant, but also what one takes their significance to be.[22]

Exactly which features of works merit critical attention has no general answer. Features which have gone unnoticed at one time, or if noticed have been regarded as unimportant, have at later times become crucial. For example, some critics have suggested that 'the syntactical incoherence of certain speeches, in e.g. *Macbeth*, may be of significance as expressive of deep and disordered trains of thought; in this way a hitherto extraneous . . . feature of the text becomes part of the play'.[23] Similarly, certain images in Shakespeare whose importance seems obvious to us now were neglected until Knight called attention to them.

Which features of a work are singled out for notice is a tensed issue, depending as it does on the factors mentioned earlier: the state of the art, the state of criticism, and the general intellectual climate.[24] Moreover, a given feature can change in significance as changes in the above circumstances occur. The following comment made about a film maker is of a type often made about other artists:

> His art had become so deceptively simple by the time of 'Abraham Lincoln' that most critics who saw the film at its release assumed he was in a state of stylistic decline. Yet today the directness of 'Lincoln' looks amazingly appropriate to its subject.[25]

I have been suggesting why any given critical perception is compatible with all sorts of further refinements. Discriminations unavailable at one time may become available as changes occur in critical interests, in the art, or in the intellectual climate. Beckett's work may enable one to make new discriminations in Shakespeare. Interest in psychoanalysis may point to previously unexplored motivational possibilities in *Othello* or *Hedda Gabler*.

But one might wonder why there should be a difficulty in setting limits when the domain is art criticism, since no such difficulty exists in a good many other domains where an unlimited number of distinctions is also theoretically possible. If we look at some cases where limits have been set although a continuum was available, we discover that the generally accepted purposes of these enterprises make it clear why it would be non-arbitrary to set some limits. For example, the light is on or off, the temperature is 72, not between 71.99 and 72, people are inner- or outer- or other-directed, not between inner- and outer-, they have oral or anal fantasies, not between oral and anal, a given pitch is one of seven or of twelve possible musical pitches, a person is driving in excess of a stated speed limit. In these cases we find that no purpose intrinsic to the activity would be served by considering all the possible intermediate positions, and moreover that purposes that are intrinsic would be frustrated by considering them.

When we turn to the domain of criticism, however, what are the generally accepted purposes of criticism? If we allow that there are some generally accepted purposes – for example, one might be determining what artworks show – do these purposes make it clear what should count as an insignificant difference in critical judgement? Indeed, isn't it a purpose of the critical enterprise to recognize and utilize the full potentialites afforded by the continuum in question? That is, although individual critics may work with limited sets of alternatives, it is always open to other critics to challenge these alternatives; the possibility of ever finer shading is always taken as a real possibility. For example, although something that Lear says may have suggested sarcasm rather than genuine beseechment to a critic, in his attempt to get at the particular shade of sarcasm, the critic might be led to abandon sarcasm for scorn. Or the critic might introduce new classifications – scornful sarcasm, scornful bathetic sarcasm, and so on. There are endless discriminations that can be made here. The history of criticism, as I said earlier, suggests that it would be a mistake for a critic to claim that he had made all the requisite ones. Although some critics may try to convince us that they have made enough, the work remains open to further scrutiny. Another look might always prove fruitful.

And another look is in order, for critics are interested not merely in, for example, Lear's general tone in approaching his daughter, but in his precise tone. The value that there is, and the interest critics have, in exploiting all the positions afforded by the continuum available to them are not, I would suggest, unlike the value and interest that attaches to exploiting intermediate positions in reading faces.

> I say, e.g. of a smile: 'It wasn't quite genuine.'
> 'Oh bosh, the lips were parted only 1/1000th of an inch too much. Does it matter?'
> 'Yes.'[26]

It is true that critics limit the alternatives they work with; a work is said to be dignified rather than pompous or ponderous, grand rather than grandiose. However, since it is possible that later scrutiny could reveal significant new subtleties in a work (and such scrutiny often does so), it seems reasonable to allow that, whatever critical terms are used with a work it is always in principle possible that the refinement of these terms, however slight, could make a significant difference in one's understanding of the work. A scornful sarcasm differs from either a warning or a demanding sarcasm, as does a scornful bathetic sarcasm from a scornful bargaining sarcasm. And these in turn differ from a sarcastic beseechment, or a bathetic beseechment, and so on.

However, if we allow that any difference can in principle make a difference, that any difference could yield a significant new alternative, then, however exact any critical term was, it would in principle be impossible to determine that it was the precisely right one. If criticism *as a whole* has as an epistemic aim not resting content with anything short of maxim precision, i.e., the precisely right term, known to be such, and if, therefore, no satisfactory general limits on critical discernment are to be drawn, then the desire to know *exactly* what properties any work expresses would be a desire which, like the carrot dangling before the donkey's nose, leads its pursuer on while managing always to elude him.[27]

I have suggested why it may be reasonable to view the critical enterprise as a whole as having absolute precision for a long term epistemic aim,[28] even if at any given stage of the enterprise critics assume limits. If such precision were a requirement for knowledge of the truth of certain interpretive claims, then, given that it would not be possible to rule out relevant counter-possibilities, it would always be possible to defeat claims to know that the statements constituting these interpretations were true. Defeat by a relevant counterpossibility of a critic's interpretive claim to know what a work expresses, is, given absolute precision, an always available mode of defeat. However, if limits are set, then, as long as one is prepared to talk about an interpretive claim being true and of a critic who has sufficient justification as knowing that what he says in it is true, the critic cannot claim to know that his claim is precisely right.

Statements and defeat by falsifying

While defeat of a critic's claim to know by showing that a relevant counterpossibility has not been ruled out is a common mode of defeat in the critical domain, defeating the critic's claim to know by showing that what he claims to know is false is a much less common phenomenon. Falsifying, we saw, defeats not only the critic's claim to know, but also the interpretive remark itself. Why, however, is it difficult in art criticism to falsify an interpretive remark, and why, when falsification does occur, does this not always result in the withdrawal of the interpretive remark?[29]

Falsification is difficult to obtain in art criticism because, as we have seen, there is no unanimity among critics with regard to the nature of an artwork and therefore no unanimity about the criteria for falsifying interpretive claims about them. For example, a Greenbergian modernist interpreting a Pollock painting denies the painting has a performance dimension; a Rosenbergian expressionist includes such a dimension.[30] Panofsky interprets the development of Gothic lettering culturally – the lettering tended to emulate the model apparent in architecture. If an historian of print provides a physical explanation – the lettering developed because of the materials available to the printer – would this latter explanation falsify Panofsky's? Is the development of Gothic lettering to be interpreted physically rather than culturally? While an interpretation which conflicted with successfully carried out authorial intent would not count for a formalist or deconstructivist towards falsifying an interpretive claim,[31] it would count toward falsifying it for other critics.

Another reason why falsification is difficult to obtain is that the evidence needed to establish falsity is frequently unavailable. As we have already seen, in a number of cases the evidence available may be compatible with contrary, yet equally warranted, interpretations.

Falsification, even when it is obtainable, need not result in the withdrawal of the interpretive claim so falsified. Defeat, as I have said, is under a description only and the interpretive claim in question may be more complex than a simple statement.[32] For example, if, in interpreting, a critic were not only stating but were also prescribing, then, even if one could show that what was stated was false and thereby defeat the statement, what was prescribed would not necessarily be defeated.

In some cases of interpreting falsifying is not difficult, it is inappropriate. Such cases are those in which the critic is not stating. He may be prescribing, or reporting a special kind of experience or . . . . I shall now consider interpretive remarks for which the statement model might not be an appropriate one.

Other statuses and other modes of defeat

In this section I want to show that the question – what status and epithet of value are appropriate for interpretive remarks? – has no simple answer. Different remarks have different statuses, take different values. Moreover, deciding how to view a particular remark – viz., as a statement about a work, an hypothesis, a report of an experience-as, a prescription, a complex of these, a characterizing remark – may not be a matter of deciding which way of viewing it is true, but rather of deciding which way of viewing it furthers one's understanding of it, given who utters it and in what circumstances.

Consider, for example, Frederick Crews' various inter-pretations of *Winnie-the-Pooh* in his book *The Pooh Perplex*. Assume that some sort of infelicity is possible with regard to these interpretations, and that they have some textual support. Shall we regard Crews as *stating* that Pooh is an 'Adamsubstitute', 'Rabbit is the capitalist manager *par excellence*,'[33] and his statements as expressing knowledge claims; or shall we regard him as *hypothesizing*, and his hypotheses as expressing plausibility claims? Or shall we view him as *prescribing* that we regard Pooh and Rabbit in these ways, not because he believes that he knows that, or believes that he knows that it is plausible that, they are these ways – it seems clear that he believes neither – but because it is amusing and instructive to do so? Since Crews is parodying ways of interpreting literary works, showing that relevant features of the story must be ignored or countered if his recommendation is to be carried out would not defeat the recommendation, but rather contribute to its success. Reason has been provided why the proper reading should be a distorted one. In these circumstances, my suggestion is that it is more instructive to regard Crews as recommending than to regard him as stating or hypothesizing.

One might ultimately want to regard the Christian interpreters of the earlier biblical texts or of Virgil, for example, as *prescribing* how these books should be read. As Frank Kermode points out with regard to the former: in the second century, 'when the old Testament finally became joined to the New' and hence 'was assured a permanent place in the Christian canon', Christian interpreters assumed that

> the more obvious senses of the Old Testament, including its historical meaning, were of small or no importance, were dangerous illusions, even. The Old Testament made sense only insofar as it prefigured Christianity. The rest of it – a great deal – was deafness, blindness, forgetfulness.[34]

That these interpreters did not view themselves as recommending a way of viewing these texts, that they believed themselves to be getting at the true meanings (the texts, like oracles, revealed their true meaning only at some later time), would not make it inappropriate to regard these interpreters as recommending. Regarding these interpreters as recommending would, I suggest, further one's understanding of these claims, and it would remove them from certain kinds of defeat. If, for example, we were to regard the interpretations of the Old

Testament given by the Christian interpreters as statements purporting to express knowledge, the interpreters' claim to know that the statements constituting their interpretations were true would be defeated, unless these interpreters could show why the non-Christian reading was not a relevant counterpossibility. Moreover, these interpretive claims would not be plausible if the distortions these claims contain could not be accounted for. That is, the Christian interpreters would have to establish the deafness, blindness, and forgetfulness of the earlier non-Christian compilers.

Alternatively, one could view these interpreters as *reporting their experiencing* of these works *as* Christian works. This way of viewing them would also have the advantage of avoiding certain obvious infelicities. It might be possible to regard the interpreters as both recommending and experiencing-as, for the experiencing-as model I described is compatible with the prescriptive model. For example, a critic can report that he has experienced the work as a Christian work and also prescribe that others do so as well.

Interpretive remarks like 'The line in Housman's poem in which "headpiece clever" occurs suggests school boy slang',[35] 'In the last movement of Schubert's D major piano sonata, the strongly contrasting passages are rather like the faces one might make to frighten children'[36] are what have been called characterizing remarks,[37] since they attempt to give a face to the work. The standard of acceptability for remarks of this sort is their success in getting others to experience the works in the terms they suggest.[38]

Even if one regards many of the interpretive remarks in art criticism as statements, one need not deny that a purpose of criticism, a purpose emphasized by the prescriptivist, is to get others to see the works in the ways in which the critic sees them, for getting others to see things as one does oneself is a common purpose of statement in general. The critic who, in interpreting, is stating must provide reasons for his statements. Reasons which serve as evidence for an interpretive claim can also serve as 'rules of action,' as guides to follow if one is to see the work aright. There is no need, therefore, to deny that 'it is a function of criticism to bring about communication at the level of the senses'.[39] Having this kind of a goal is consistent with making statements about the work.

Criticism would be otiose if the readers of criticism did not try to detect for themselves those features critically ascribed to artworks, whatever the status of the critical ascriptions. Is Pamela a virtuous virgin, or a sly, crafty, hypocritical girl? Can she be both? How does one tell whether a critic who states, or who hypothesizes, that she is a virtuous virgin is entitled to make either a knowledge claim or a plausibility claim about the work? Alternatively, if the critic were recommending that she be regarded as a virtuous virgin, how do we tell whether his recommendation can be obeyed? Or, if he is taken as reporting on his experience of her as a virtuous virgin, how would we decide whether his is a genuine seeing-as experience? Not by relying on critical authority, but by reading the book and trying to see whether what is stated is the case, or what is hypothesized is plausible, or whether what is recommended can be done, or whether one can in fact have the requisite experience-as.[40]

I have claimed that the supposition that interpretive remarks are statements (although not all interpretive remarks need be statements) does justice to significant features of critical practice and allows us to explain – without ruling out multiple interpretations – how critics can confront and significantly defeat one another. In the next chapter I consider whether this supposition allows us to distinguish between interpreting and describing.

Notes

1 I associate plausibility-claiming exclusively with hypothesizing to facilitate characterizing what I take to be Joseph Margolis' position.
2 Critics may not, of course, be aware of the difference between defeating an utterance *qua* interpretive remark and defeating the utterance *qua* knowledge claim and hence they may not be aware of what their challenges accomplish.
3 I am making use in this discussion of defeating a knowledge claim of distinctions put forth by Richard Warner in his presented paper 'Subjectivity and objectivity.'
4 A counterpossibility to the claim to know that p is 'a (logically possible) state of affairs S such that it is not logically possible for p

and S to jointly obtain'. 'A state of affairs S is a *relevant* counterpossibility to the claim to know that p if and only if S is a counterpossibility to that claim, and the claimant has an adequate justification for thinking that p only if he has an adequate justification for thinking that S does not obtain.' Warner notes that 'it is not at all clear that every counterpossibility to a knowledge claim is a relevant counterpossibility'.

5 Although I discuss only one seemingly possible analogue here and show why it is not a possible one, I would argue that no plausible analogue is possible.

6 While some prescriptions could thus be ruled out, those who represent critical interpretations as prescriptions argue that acceptable prescriptions will not, however, be limited to one. Cf. Charles Stevenson, 'Interpretation and evaluation in aesthetics', in Kennick, ed. *Art and Philosophy* (1st edn), 483: 'No matter how inexorably its scientific aspects are subject to the canons of inductive and deductive logic, it will bring with it no conclusions that impose a uniformity on the way in which a work of art must be observed. It may – indeed, it *does* rule out certain of these ways, since no one, in the light of knowledge, is content to decide in their favor. But it will not rule out all ways but one.' Prescriptions in art criticism, therefore, do not require that the prescription be *the* way the most discriminating critic would regard *x*, for such a standard would rule out all ways but one.

7 M. Kinkead Weekes in his introduction to Richardson's novel (London, 1966) pp. v–xiii discusses whether Pamela is a virtuous virgin or an hypocritical, crafty girl.

8 Although we are assuming for the sake of example that being a virtuous virgin is not compatible with craft and hypocrisy, this assumption itself could be questioned. Could not a virtuous virgin have some measure of craft and hypocrisy? Jane Austin in *Emma*, for example, presents comparable ambiguities. Should we view Emma as truly innocent of Mr Elton's matrimonial intentions towards her, so that her actions were entirely misinterpreted by him? or is she self-deceived about her own actions and actually encouraging him? Neither alternative may be quite right since there may be some admixture of self-deceit and innocence.

If it were possible for critics to regard Pamela in each of these two ways, although it was not possible for a single critic to regard her in both simultaneously, then this could shed light on each of the separate ways. For this possibility could draw attention to the fact that in those situations where such easy confusion is possible, it may be difficult or impossible to decide between the two ways unless further constraints upon the prescriptions are imposed. One might, for example, want to regard her in the way that does not conflict with the author's executed intention, or with historical information about how she was regarded by her contemporary readers, or . . . That is, if it were relevant and significant that Richardson intended *Pamela* to be a primer for feminine virtue rather than an ironic commentary on that virtue, or that his contemporaries took it as such a primer and Richardson did not protest, then one might have a way of deciding between these interpretations.

9 'Joint obeyance' means that each of them can be obeyed. Obeying one prescription does not make it impossible to obey the other. A single critic could not regard Pamela in both these ways simultaneously, although he could regard her in one of the ways on one occasion and in the other way on another occasion, *if* Pamela could not simultaneously be both of these ways. An analogue to a relevant counterpossibility does not require that a single critic jointly obey the prescriptions, viz., obey them simultaneously. Defeat by a relevant counterpossibility occurs in the interchange between critics. One critic says 'Pamela is a virtuous virgin.' Another critic protests 'No, she is a crafty, hypocritical girl.' If interpretive statements were knowledge claims, a relevant question would be whether 'it is true that Pamela is a virtuous virgin' urged by one critic and 'it is true that Pamela is a crafty, hypocritical girl' urged by another critic could jointly be true. If interpretive remarks were prescriptions, a relevant question is whether 'regard her as a virtuous virgin' suggested by one critic and 'regard her as a crafty, hypocritical girl' suggested by another critic could jointly be obeyed. If, as we assumed, each of the prescriptions is an obeyable one, then two equally discriminating critics could jointly obey them, i.e., obey them simultaneously.

10 This controversy is cited in Radford and Minogue, *The Nature of Criticism*, p. 55ff.

11 Ibid., p. 58.

12 Ibid. The critic quoted is Christopher Ricks.

13 If interpretations were reports of special kinds of experience, then one would talk about the work's aspects; if interpretations were hypotheses, then one would talk of imputing properties to the work, if interpretations were prescriptions, one would talk about the ways the work should be regarded.

14 F. R. Leavis in *The Common Pursuit* cited in *The Nature of Criticism* makes a claim akin to this, pp. 57–58.

15 Stanley Cavell, *Must We Mean What We Say?*, p. 311.

16 E. D. Hirsch is the critic. This quote appears in Fish's *Is There a*

Text in This Class?, p. 339. Kathleen Paine is said to give an interpretation which entails that the tiger is evil.

17 Roger Scruton, *Art and Imagination*, pp. 178–9. I am supposing, as Scruton would not, that the critics involved here are claiming to know that the music is one or another way and are not reporting on their hearing-as experiences.

18 For example, in an exchange concerning Ford's *The Good Soldier*, Frank Kermode finds '*saddest* is a bit lame, perhaps, and certainly misleading', while Denis Donoghue believes '*saddest* is all right, because Dowell is presented as the kind of man to whom *mezzo-forte* terms of description come naturally; even his superlatives sound like comparatives'. Denis Donogue, 'A reply to Frank Kermode, *Critical Inquiry* no. 1 (December 1974); 450.

Stuart Hampshire in 'Types of interpretation', *Art and Philosophy* edited by Sidney Hook (New York, 1966), 101–8, suggested that 'the two most plausible candidates for an illuminating analogy to critical interpretation', are 'the interpretation of dreams and secondly, the interpretation that an actor or musician gives. They are widely different types of interpretation, and different types of criticism will show an analogy with one rather than the other.' When the critic is functioning in a manner analogous to the actor or musician, the critic according to Hampshire must be minutely exact. For, 'he who interprets a role or a piece of music has narrow limits within which he must move. He must stay as close as he can to the text, and only then can he find different shades of emphasis, different phrasing, which he may choose, or which may come naturally to his temperament.' The literary critic, who functions analogously, 'in all questions of pure aesthetic quality . . . has to be minutely exact. He makes one see (hear, notice, while reading) the exact calculation of intervals, the pauses, transitions, juxtapositions, omissions.' The demand for precision occurs because 'a shade of emphasis may well make all the difference in bringing out what is there in the text'.

19 Cf. Nelson Goodman, *Languages of Art*, p. 135ff where the notion of finite differentiation is discussed.

20 The measurement analogue – between ironic forgiveness and mocking forgiveness there is that forgiveness which we can describe as 'the forgiveness between ironic and mocking forgiveness', and between this forgiveness . . . is only one model for creating an unlimited number of distinctions. Increasing specificity by the use of adjectival modifiers is another. A third is to show that a difference in emphasis in an interpretation at any one point may influence interpretations of the work as a whole or interpretations of other

parts of the work. The number of these latter kinds of interpretation is not limited. Moreover, the difference in emphasis of an interpretation at any one point is related in an unlimited number of ways to these other interpretations. Hence an unlimited number of distinctions are possible.

21 Goodman calls a system semantically dense, as is a natural language, when 'it provides for an infinite number of characters with compliance-classes so ordered that between each two there is a third'. (*Languages of Art*, p. 153) Natural language thus provides for (there does not actually have to be) a dense set of compliance classes as well as providing for an unlimited number of characters.

22 For example, in Beckett's comedy of outrage, the *risus puris* – the laugh that laughs at that which is unhappy – requires one to view both the fury of impotency and the impotence of fury as funny.

23 Richard Wollheim, *Art and Its Objects*, pp. 76–7.

24 For discussion of this see *Art and Its Objects*, pp. 76–9.

25 'He transcended technique', an article about D. W. Griffith, *New York Times* (19 January 1975), 15.

26 Ludwig Wittgenstein, *Lectures and Conversations on Aesthetics, Psychology and Religious Belief* (Berkeley, 1966) Cyril Barrett, ed., p. 31.

27 Goodman argues that the systems of literary exemplification and expression are semantically dense (*Languages of Art*, pp. 238–40). The density of these systems explains why 'endless search is always required here (in literature) as in other arts to determine precisely what is exemplified and expressed'. (p. 240). For 'where there is density in the symbol system, familiarity is never complete and final; another look may always disclose significant new subtleties'. (p. 260).

   In a system which is semantically dense what he refers to as the requirements of semantic finite differentiation is everywhere violated. This latter requirement holds that '*for every two characters K and K' and every object h that does not comply with both, determination either that h does not comply with K or that h does not comply with K' must be theoretically possible*'. (pp. 152–3). I have tried to show why in criticism the requirement of semantic finite differentiation is not satisfiable. Both K and K' are words. Failure to satisfy this requirement means that no work or passage or line could be determined to comply with at most one character. Density, however, 'is not implied by absence of differentiation throughout'. (p. 227n) I refer the reader to Goodman's arguments for the semantic density of natural language, literary exemplification, and literary expression. This density, I would agree, 'arises out of, and sustains, the unsatisfiable demand for absolute precision'. (p. 253).

28 Some might argue that the demand for absolute precision is an inappropriate or unintelligible demand in art criticism for this demand assumes that artworks can have absolutely precise expressions in a manner analogous to tables having absolutely precise lengths. If artworks can not have absolutely precise expressive properties, then the demand for absolute precision is misguided. On this view, it would be unreasonable to suppose that there is an absolutely precise answer in cases of expression; there would, for example, be no precisely right expression attachable to Lear's utterance, 'on my knees . . . '. While it would be true that the absolutely precise answer would be unknowable, it would be unknowable because there would be no precisely right answer to be known.

In this discussion I have assumed that it is plausible to think that a demand for absolute precision in the domain of art criticism with regard to expressive properties is not an inappropriate or unintelligible demand, linking the case of artistic expression to the case of facial expression and linking the coherence of critical practice as a whole with regard to expression to this demand. The issue is further complicated by the fact that an artwork's expressive properties may be relative to time, place, comparison class, to what is literally true of the work, and so on. The question would then be whether it makes sense to think of any art work as having an exact expression in a particular context, although, given my argument, one would not be able to know what that exact expression was.

While the claim I make in this discussion could be true whether or not there was any demand for absolute precision with respect to expressive properties – I claim that *if* there were such a demand, it could not be satisfied – my claim would be an idle one if there were no demand for absolute precision. I leave the reader to decide whether my assumption of plausibility with regard to this demand is justified here and hence whether my claim is a fruitful one.

29 Anita Silvers brought these features about falsification to my attention. She is responsible for the Panofsky example I use.
30 Noel Carroll suggested this example.
31 Some may claim that there is no 'successfully carried out artistic intent'.
32 Anita Silvers suggested this possibility.
33 Frederick Crews, *The Pooh Perplex* (New York, 1963), pp. 56, 21.
34 Frank Kermode, *The Genesis of Secrecy* (Cambridge, 1980), p. 18.
35 Radford and Minogue, *The Nature of Criticism*, p. 63.

36 Denis Dutton, 'Plausibility and aesthetic interpretation', *Canadian Journal of Philosophy*, vol. II, no. 2 (June 1977) cites this example.

37 Radford and Minogue, *The Nature of Criticism*, p. 49.

38 Ibid., p. 64.

39 Arnold Isenberg, 'Critical communication', *Art and Philosophy* Kennick ed., (2nd edn), 663.

40 T. S. Eliot, 'The frontiers of criticism', *On Poetry and Poets* (New York, 1964), 131. 'So the critic to whom I am most grateful is the one who can make me look at something I have never looked at before, or looked at only with eyes clouded by prejudice, set me face to face with it and then leave me alone with it. From that point, I must rely upon my own sensibility, intelligence, and capacity for wisdom.'

8

Interpreting and Describing

I have argued that in order to interpret x as F for oneself, one must not know$_k$ that x is F. This link between not knowing$_k$ and interpreting for oneself is a general one; 'x' need not be limited to artworks. Regarding artworks, whatever status an interpretation of x enjoys — whether it is a statement, an hypothesis, a prescription, a report of a special kind of experience — if one is interpreting x as F for oneself, then one does not know$_k$ that x is literally or figuratively F.

If an interpretation were a prescription, then the difference between describing and interpreting would be readily apparent. A prescription, unlike a description, would not be a statement, it would not take the values 'true' and 'false', nor would it claim that the object in question, x, had a property, F. However, when an interpretation is a statement, the difference between interpreting and describing is not so readily apparent. Since I have argued that regarding many interpretive remarks as statements does justice to important features of critical practice, I want to consider whether, when an interpretation is a statement, interpreting can be distinguished from describing. Initially the discussion will not be limited to artworks.

If a necessary condition for interpreting for oneself is not already knowing$_k$, then interpreting for oneself differs in this regard from describing. That is,

(A) In order for A to interpret x as F for himself:
    (1) It must be the case that A does not know$_k$ that x is F.

(B) In order for A to describe x as F:

    (1) It need not be the case that A does not know$_k$ whether x is F.

Given conditions (1), when A does not know$_k$ whether x is F, it is possible for A either to interpret x as F for himself or to describe x as F. How, in these circumstances, does one determine which of the activities is occurring? Matthews suggests,[1] we saw, that:

> In order for A to interpret x as F for himself, it must be the case that A is not in a position to know whether x is F. In order for A to describe x as F, it must be the case that A is in a position to know whether x is F.

Is either of Matthews' conditions correct? I believe that neither is, for one can interpret for oneself when one is in a position to know and one can describe when one is not in a position to know.

For example, suppose on the evidence available in *Death of a Salesman* a critic would be in a position to know whether Willy Loman was deceiving himself about his opportunity to go to Alaska with his brother Ben, but, due to an oversight, a particular critic was not aware of it. If, however, the critic was led by other considerations, e.g., Willy's general pattern of deception, to the view that Willy is deceiving himself here, then although the critic was in a position to know this about Willy, since he didn't know it, he was able to interpret this for himself.

A person would be in a position to know how many words (word tokens) begin with 'mo' in the unexpurgated edition of *Sister Carrie*, if he had the complete text before him, could read, and was able to count. If, however, a person used a defective copy of the text – a page was missing – then he would not be in a position to know whether his answer was correct. His answer might be correct, nevertheless, if, for example, the missing page had no 'mo' words on it. In such a case the critic would be describing, rather than interpreting for himself.

If Matthews' conditions are inadequate, then how does one determine which cases of not knowing$_k$ whether x is F are cases of interpreting x as F for oneself and which are cases of describing? Is it ever possible, for example, for a person to be doing both? If we also take into account interpreting for others, the issue becomes more complicated, for whereas interpreting for oneself can be distinguished from some cases of describing in terms of not knowing$_k$, not knowing$_k$ is not a requirement for interpreting for others. That is:

> (C) In order for A to interpret x as F for others:
> (1) It need not be the case that A does not know$_k$ whether x is F.

This condition is the same as that for describing.

Although when one interprets x as F for others, one is not required not to know$_k$ whether x is F, I believe that it is required that the people for whom one interprets do not know$_k$ that x is F. I do not, for example, interpret Willy's behavior as self-deceptive for you if you already know$_k$ that it is. No such requirement on the intended audience is present in describing. We have, therefore, the following additional condition for interpreting for others which allows us to distinguish it from some cases of describing:

> (C) In order for A to interpret x as F for others:
> (2) It must be the case that there are others, for whom one interprets, who do not know$_k$ that x is F.

Given that an interpretation can be either for oneself or for others, to determine whether a given statement is an interpretation one must know the epistemic condition of both the speaker and his audience (if any). If this is correct, then not only, as some philosophers have suggested, may the same words uttered by one person be an interpretation and uttered by another not be an interpretation (cf. Kennick and Matthews), it can also be the case that 'x is F' uttered by a given person may be an interpretation if we are talking about interpreting for oneself, and not an interpretation if we are talking about interpreting for others. The status of 'x is F' as description does not undergo similar changes.

How, then, are we to determine whether describing or interpreting for oneself or for others is occurring in those cases where the not knowing$_k$ requirement is not sufficient to rule out one of the activities? There is no easy way to determine this.

Although I mention one further necessary condition for interpreting, since it is necessary for both interpreting and describing, it will not help one to distinguish between them. And various other conditions that have looked promising either as individually necessary or sufficient for one or the other activity, are neither individually necessary or sufficient. We may have to settle for sets of conditions, each of which is sufficient for one or the other activity, although none is necessary.

I shall first look briefly at some initially plausible conditions. It is generally agreed that people with at least certain minimum capacities and abilities, i.e., people with normal eyes, ears, intelligence, etc., have access to features of a large number of objects. It might seem plausible to suppose that when one classifies an object in ways that are generally known$_k$ or that could be easily known$_k$ by anyone with minimum knowledge and skills, then one is describing the object rather than interpreting it. Something analogous to this condition is perhaps suggested by the philosopher who claims that in describing the emphasis is on 'a stable object whose properties are enumerable (however complex they may be)' while in interpreting it is on 'an object whose properties pose something of a puzzle or challenge'.[2] What is easily or generally known$_k$ does not ordinarily present something of a puzzle or challenge.

Classifying an object in a way that is already generally known$_k$, or easily knowable$_k$, is not, however, a sufficient condition for describing. Classifying an object in a way that is not already known$_k$ or easily knowable$_k$ is not a necessary condition for interpreting either for oneself or for others. It could happen that through an oversight a person did not know$_k$ that a character was deceiving himself, although this fact was generally known$_k$, or could be easily known about the character. In such a case the person would have room to interpret this for himself. A critic could interpret the figure in a painting as a nude woman for a non-Western viewer unfamiliar with representational works.

Nor is classifying an object in a way that is already generally known$_k$ or easily knowable$_k$ a necessary condition for describing (or classifying an object in a way that is not already generally known$_k$ or easily knowable$_k$ is not a sufficient condition for interpreting for oneself or for others) Suppose Clarence knows$_k$ that Clarissa counts waves, although this is not an easily knowable$_k$, or generally known$_k$, fact about her. When he characterizes her for himself or for his friends as 'a woman who counts waves' it seems clear that he is describing her either to himself or to them, not interpreting her.

Mark Sagoff, in his discussion of describing and interpreting in art criticism, suggests that if one classifies artworks in ways that stay within established reference classes, it is plausible to speak of describing, whereas, if one goes outside such classes, it is plausible to speak of interpreting.

> Notice that an *interpretation*, in so far as it can be said to differ from a *description*, differs in emphasis or purpose. It not only describes relational features of an object, let us say an art object, but it tends to go outside entrenched reference classes in order to focus attention on aesthetically interesting relations between the objects and others with which it is not usually associated.[3]

He points out that *King Lear* 'is a moral tragedy in relation to Elizabethan histories, comedies, and tragedies; when studied in relation to Sam Beckett's plays . . . it has many qualities of the drama of the absurd'.[4] The suggestion seems to be that to classify *King Lear* as a tragedy is to describe *Lear*; to classify it as a drama of the absurd is to interpret it.

Sagoff does not claim to be providing either a necessary or a sufficient condition for the description or the interpretation of art objects, so he could presumably agree with what I shall go on to claim. I shall claim that (1) going outside entrenched categories is not necessary for interpreting for oneself or others (staying within entrenched categories is not sufficient for describing), and (2) going outside entrenched categories is not sufficient for interpreting for oneself or others (not going outside entrenched categories is not necessary for describing).

Deciding how many characters are in a play may, as in the case of *Waiting for Godot*, require interpretive effort. If one is tempted to say five – Estragon, Vladimir, Lucky, Posso, a boy – it can be pointed out that 'a boy' may be two characters. Given the convention that the same actor can play more than one role, and given that there is some evidence within the play to suggest that there might be two different messenger boys, could there not be six characters? Since the critic who says that there are five characters cannot rule out the possibility that there are six, he cannot claim to know$_k$ that there are five. He could, therefore, be interprting for himself as well as interpreting for others. Moreover, he has not gone outside established reference classes, as he would have done if he had introduced a non-standard way of individuating characters – for example, if he had introduced pseudo-couples, where Estragon-Vladimir and Posso-Lucky count as two and not as four characters. (1) is, therefore, true.

The critic who classifies *Endgame* as a comedy, in a novel sense of 'comedy', when he knows$_k$ that *Endgame* is one is not interpreting this for himself. I am assuming that the predicate 'comedy' is not only a novel predicate, but also a projectable one. If others know that *Endgame* is a comedy of this sort, then he is not interpreting for them. He is, however, going outside established reference classes. Thus (2) is true: going outside entrenched categories is not sufficient for interpreting.

I have described certain conditions, but since these conditions are not individually necessary or sufficient for interpreting or describing, it could happen that two situations, similarly characterized with regard to these conditions, involved two different activities. For example, consider the case in which a critic who has overlooked some relevant evidence is trying to decide whether Willy Loman is deceiving himself. In this situation:

(1) The critic does not know that Willy is deceiving himself.
(2) The critic stays within established categories.
(3) The way of classifying Willy as self-deceived is generally known$_k$ or easily knowable$_k$ by others (suppose it requires only minimal knowledge and skills to find out how old Willy was when his brother left).

Now consider the case of the person using a defective text who is trying to discover how many words beginning with 'mo' there are in *Sister Carrie*. In this situation:

(1) The person does not know how many words begin with 'mo'.
(2) The person stays within established categories.

(3) The way of classifying, although not generally known$_k$, is easily knowable$_k$ by others. (If people were generally interested in such things, then it could be generally known$_k$).

Similar conditions obtain in both these cases, yet in the first case we speak of interpreting for oneself, in the second of describing. Some other factor is relevant here. What might it be?

In the self-deception case, if the critic had read more carefully, he would have known$_k$ that the character was deceiving himself. However, since he read with less care, a decisive piece of evidence was unknown to him. He believed under these circumstances that some decision about x being F, had to be made; he had to decide whether the evidence he had warranted this characterization.

In the counting case a procedure existed which if correctly followed would have allowed a person to know$_k$ that his answer was correct. The person was, moreover, following this procedure, and had it not been for the missing page would have known$_k$ his answer to be correct. Nothing more would have been required of him. Since he was unware of the defect in the text, he was also unaware that he did not know$_k$ x to be F. He believed, therefore, that no decision about x being F was required.

These remarks suggest that if A believes that he does not have a decision to make about whether x is F (as in the counting case) – since he believes that he had by correctly following a specifiable procedure unequivocally established that x is F – then A is describing. If A believes, rightly or wrongly, that some decision about whether x is F is necessary (as in the Loman case) – A believes that the evidence does not univocally establish that x is F, further deliberation and decision is required – then A is interpreting for himself.

However, as we saw earlier, A can be interpreting for himself even if he does not believe that any decision about whether x is F is required. Recall the critic who claimed that *The Turn of the Screw* was a ghost story. Given this kind of case I must complicate the conditions: If either (1) A believes that some decision about whether x is F has to be made (for example, A believes that it cannot be univocally established that x is F given the evidence that he has, further deliberation and decision is required), or (2) that x is F cannot be univocally established given the evidence available, further deliberation and decision is required (and this deliberation may or may not result in its being established that x is F), then A is interpreting for himself.

If (1) A does not believe that some decision about whether x is F has to be made, and if (2) that x is F can be univocally established on the evidence available, then A is describing.

Let us look more closely at this latest condition for interpreting for oneself. The condition is satisfied if at least one of its alternatives is. In the self-deception case alternative (1) is satisfied, but (2) is not. In *The Turn of The Screw*-as-a-ghost-story case, (2) is satisfied, but (1) is not. However, the condition as stated needs further clarification. In particular, I have to specify what is to count as 'the evidence available' in alternative (2).

Suppose I stipulate that it is the evidence that anyone with the requisite knowledge and skills would obtain at the time provided that he was not using a defective object – e.g., no pages were missing, no part of the canvas was damaged, etc. – and that he did the required work without error. On this understanding of 'the evidence available', the evidence available in the counting case happened to coincide with the evidence on which the counter proceeded, although the counter did not use a non-defective object. In this case, therefore, alternative (2) of the condition for interpreting for oneself is not satisfied.

This condition is not, however, necessary for interpreting for oneself. That is, if it can be univocally established by the evidence available that x is F, and A does not believe that any decision about whether x is F is required, it is still possible that A is interpreting for himself and not describing. Although in cases like the counting case where neither alternative is satisfied one is describing, consider the following. Suppose A mistakenly believes that, on the evidence he has, he can establish that a character is delaying. Consequently, A doesn't believe that any decision about whether x is F is required. Suppose, moreover, that evidence is available to establish this about the character. I believe that in this case we would regard A as interpreting, for although evidence for univocally establishing that x is F existed, in the sense that evidence to this effect was available, A was not basing his claim on adequate evidence. In this particular regard he is like the critic who thinks he has univocally established a story as a ghost story when he has not.

Moreover, the conjunction of this condition with the not-knowing$_k$ condition would not be sufficient for interpreting for oneself. A person who is asked to describe his ideal mate may not know that his classifications are correct. It could also happen that given the evidence available, he would not be able, without further deliberation and decision, to establish which features his ideal mate would have and that we would yet speak of this person as describing, and not interpreting, his ideal mate. This example also shows that the condition is not sufficient for interpreting for others.

Nor is the condition necessary for interpreting for others. Consider the critic who interprets a figure in a representational work for someone who is initially unable to read it.

Although I have allowed that A could describe x as F even if A's description contained a claim about meaning or significance – A can describe Willy as self-deceived, *Lear* as a tragedy – is it possible for A to interpret x as F if A's interpretation does not contain a claim about meaning? Many philosophers have thought it was not possible. It is, says Matthews, 'a necessary condition for something's being an interpretation that the statements constituting the interpretation make claims about the meaning, import, value, significance, etc. of the interpretandum'.[5] 'The statement "the painting includes a mauve elliptical area" is, as a matter of fact, typically descriptive, since critics are not given to conjecturing. (It cannot for logical reasons be interpretive.)'[6] Is Matthews right?

Imagine that A, a red–green color blind person, is looking at a painting in which there is a red patch. A, given his defect, cannot tell that the patch is red merely by looking. If, however, A concludes that it is red – he decides that given the kind of representation it is, a red but not a green patch is statistically more likely, or given what he knows about the colors the painter usually puts together, a green but not a red patch is more likely – wouldn't A be interpreting the patch as red for himself, not merely conjecturing or guessing that it is, and also not describing it as such? (I am assuming that A doesn't know that it is red.) If

A were addressing an audience of similarly color blind people, would he not also be interpreting this for them? If we answer 'yes' to both of the above, then making some claim about the meaning, import, etc., of *x* is not a necessary condition for interpreting.

Some philosophers have suggested that when A is interpreting *x*, A must be explaining *x*. Kennick, for example, suggests that an interpretation, 'or at least one kind of interpretation – would seem to be a species of explanation whose function is to aid understanding and appreciation'.[7]

Is it the case that if A is interpreting *x* as *F*, A must be explaining *x*? The first thing to notice here is that whether a given remark is an explanation depends upon the context, what question is being asked, what the questioner knows. Just as in certain contexts a description can be an explanation, so in certain contexts an interpretation can be an explanation.

Whether all interpreting must be explaining, or all interpretations explanations, however, depends upon how one understands explaining or explanation. If, for example, by 'explaining' one means explaining why, i.e., if in explaining one is answering a why-question – 'Why is *x* as it is?' – then clearly not all interpreting is explaining.[8] The critic who interpreted a character as having three daughters was not, in the circumstances I stipulated, explaining why the character had three daughters. One could, of course, imagine other contexts in which the remark, 'the character has three daughters', could count as an explanation why. For example, suppose a person wanted to know why the character was cantankerous. The critic answered, 'the character has three daughters!', the presumption, however dubious, being that given what daughters are like, having three of them is enough to make any parent cantankerous.

However, not all requests for explanation involve why-questions. Some may call for answers to what-questions. 'Explain a fugue' may be a request for an explanation of what a fugue is, and not for an explanation of why it is as it is. If explanation is used in the wider sense to cover both explanation what and explanation why, then it is trivially true that all interpretation is also explanation. I shall in the discussion following use 'explaining' to refer to explaining why.

Although I have not come up with any further significant conditions which are individually necessary or sufficient, it seems that when:

(1) A does not know$_k$ that x is F;
(2) A is classifying in ways not already generally known$_k$ or easily knowable$_k$ by anyone with minimum knowledge and skills;
(3) A is classifying in ways that go outside entrenched reference classes;
(4) Either A believes that a decision about whether x is F is required given the evidence he has, or that x is F cannot be univocally established on the evidence available, further deliberation and decision being required;
(5) A is making some claim about the meaning of x;[9]
(6) A is explaining x (explaining why x is as it is); and
(7) A has evidential support for his belief that x is F;

A is interpreting x as F for himself. Condition (7) is needed in order to rule out conjecturing or guessing. This condition is necessary, therefore, for both interpreting and describing. These conditions seem jointly sufficient for interpreting for oneself; no counterexample is forthcoming. Counterexamples to subsets of these conditions can, in contrast, be found. For example, a man who describes his ideal mate could on some occasion satisfy all but condition (5). However, I do not claim to have discussed all the conditions that might be relevant for deciding whether one is describing or interpreting. Some subsets of these conditions together with some other condition(s) would also be jointly sufficient for interpreting for oneself.

When (1) through (7), or (2) through (7), hold, and A is addressing an audience that does not know$_k$ that x is F, then it seems that A is interpreting x as F for others. When, on the other hand:

(8) A knows$_k$ that x is F;
(9) A is classifying in ways already generally known$_k$, or easily knowable$_k$, by anyone with minimum knowledge and skills;
(10) A is classifying in ways that stay within entrenched reference classes;

(11) A doesn't believe that any further decision about whether x is F is required, and that x is F can be univocally established on the evidence available;

(12) A is not making some claim about the meaning of x;

(13) A is not explaining x (explaining why x is as it is); and

(14) A has evidential support for his belief that x is F;

it seems that A is describing x as F. When (9) through (14) hold it also seems sufficient that A is describing x as F.

Although interpreting for oneself or others frequently involves choosing, interpreting does not entail choosing. Even when a choice is available, if A is unaware of it, A is not choosing; a person is choosing only when that person is aware of doing so. A similar requirement is not placed on interpreting.

Interpreting and choosing are distinguishable activities. Neither entails the other, but nothing prevents an activity in certain circumstances from being both choosing and interpreting. Is there a similar compatibility between interpreting and describing?

To a certain extent, it is clear that describing and interpreting are not mutually exclusive activities. That is, when A $knows_k$ that x is F, his activity can be describing x as F and yet, if his audience does not $know_k$ that x is F, his activity can at the same time be interpreting x as F for them. Similarly, if A doesn't $know_k$ that x is F, but his audience does, his activity may be interpreting x as F for himself, but describing x as F for them.

However, what about describing for oneself and interpreting for oneself, or describing for others and interpreting for others? Are these compatible? Matthews' conditions held them to be incompatible. Do the conditions I have discussed do the same?

The one condition necessary for interpreting for oneself but not necessary for describing – the condition of not $knowing_k$ – does not rule out the possibility that sometimes an activity is both interpreting for oneself and describing. Nor does it rule out the possibility that the activity of interpreting for oneself is always describing. For example, if we consider the relation between describing and explaining, we see that while not all describing is explaining, all explaining is describing. Is the relation between interpreting and describing similar in this regard to that between explaining and describing? That is, are interpreting and describing not only compatible (as are choosing and interpreting), but linked by a one-way entailment relation?

How one answers this question depends upon how broadly or narrowly one construes describing. This suggests that the question is not ultimately an interesting one. That is, if one construes describing narrowly, if only certain classifying using verbal labels is describing – e.g., that classifying which uses entrenched predicates, or that classifying which is able univocally to establish its classifications, etc. – and if only certain classifying is interpreting – e.g., that classifying which uses novel predicates, which is not able univocally to establish its classifications, etc. – then one could set up interpreting for oneself and describing for oneself as mutually exclusive kinds of classifying. If one did, the critic who *interprets* Willy as self-deceived would not simultaneously *describe* him as self-deceived. That the conditions I discussed do not provide individually necessary or sufficient conditions, does not prevent one from setting up two mutually exclusive classes, even if there is no simple way to determine which activities belong in which class.

If one construes describing broadly, if describing is any classifying using verbal labels having singular, multiple or null reference, then all interpreting done using words would necessarily also be describing. One could, however, distinguish between interpreting and describing by making interpreting a special kind of describing. For example, the describing that involved novel predicates, or which made some claim about meaning, or . . . would be interpreting, while the classifying done using established predicates which did not make some claim about meaning, . . . would be describing. Sagoff takes this latter approach for he talks of interpretation as *describing* relational features, so that for him interpreting is the describing which tends to go outside entrenched reference classes. 'In this way interpretations are descriptions which serve to enhance our critical perception and appreciation of works of art.'[10] Given the discussion so far, it does not seem to matter whether we construe describing broadly or narrowly since a distinction between describing and interpreting is possible on either construal.

Notes

1 Robert Matthews, 'Describing and interpreting a work of art', 8, 7.
2 Joseph Margolis, *Art & Philosophy*, p. 111.
3 Mark Sagoff, 'Historical authenticity', 88.
4 Ibid., 87–8.
5 Matthews, 'Describing and interpreting a work of art', 9.
6 Ibid., 10.
7 William Kennick, *Art and Philosophy* (2nd edn), p. 372.
8 Cf. G. A. Cohen, *Karl Marx's Theory of History: A Defence* (Oxford, 1978), pp. 251–3 where he distinguishes between explanations that answer *why-questions* and explanations that answer *what-questions*.
9 I have narrowed Matthews' condition in order to rule out as a counterexample the man who describes his ideal mate.
10 Sagoff, 'Historical authenticity', 88.

9

Interpreting and Diverse
Critical Activities

Before turning to the central issue of this chapter, consider again some of the salient features of interpreting. According to the account I propose in the preceding chapters, whether a critic is interpreting, and for whom, depends upon the epistemic position of both the critic and the critic's audience. The critic's own lack of knowledge is a necessary condition of his interpreting for himself; his audience's lack of knowledge is a necessary condition of his interpreting for them.

When, for example, a critic knows$_k$ that the utterances constituting his interpretation are true, but his audience do not, he can be interpreting for them, but not for himself. In such a case the critic may be like a herald proclaiming an evident sense[1] (the critic who characterizes the opening of the "Pleni sunt coeli" of Bach's *Mass in B minor* as joyful[2]); like a diviner (or insider) declaring a secret sense[3] (the critic who identifies the three beasts in Canto I of the *Inferno* as 'the main forces of evil in the world, the leopard, or lust, the lion, or pride, and the wolf, or covetousness'[4]); or like a knowledgeable translator rendering the terms of an unfamiliar language into those of a familiar one[5] (the critic who tells us the woman carrying a plate of severed breasts represents St Agnes,[6] or the critic who paraphrases the opening lines of Keat's 'Ode to Melancholy', 'No, no: go not to Lethe, neither twist / Wolf's-bane, tight-rooted, for its poisonous wine: / Nor suffer thy pale forehead to be kissed / By nightshade, ruby grape of Proserpine- . . .' as 'a parody, by contradiction, of the wise advise of uncles. "Of course, pain is what we all desire, and

I am sure I hope you will be very unhappy. But if you go snatching at it before your time, my boy, you must expect the consequences; you will hardly get hurt at all." '[7])

If a critic is interpreting rather than conjecturing or guessing, he must be able to provide reasons for his interpretation. For example, to support a claim that a work by Berlioz has the quality of unexpectedness a critic might point to 'the formidably slow and deliberative pace of certain progressions, whose final goal cannot be guessed'.

If a critic is interpreting rather than describing, then it is likely that he is not classifying in a way generally or easily known$_k$, that he is making some claim about the meaning or significance of the object interpreted, and so on. Further information is required if one wants to know whether a critic, in interpreting, is stating, prescribing, reporting a special experience, ...

In this chapter I consider what objects (when one restricts 'objects' to art objects) are subject to critical interpretations and whether the interpreting done by critics in the various arts consists of multiple activities or of a single activity with multiple types of object.

While some philosophers believe that only certain artworks are subject to interpretation – for example, it has been said that a Grandma Moses, a Currier and Ives print, the usual portraits of Matisse, a simple lyric, or paintings which are not allegorical or linked to stories,[8] are inappropriate objects of interpretation – other philosophers have argued that any artwork is subject to interpretation.[9]

I shall adopt the view that any artwork is an appropriate object of interpretation. I then focus on the different kinds of questions interpreting critics can ask, differentiating kinds of critical activities in terms of the kinds of questions asked.

If, as I believe, different objects – for example, a fugue and a piece of programme music – can pose different critical questions, then different objects can be the focus of different critical activities. On my account, interpreting is irreducibly pluralistic: fundamentally diverse critical activities count as interpreting. What specific activity or activities a given interpreting critic is engaged in depends in part upon the particular object with which he is dealing; Kafka's *The Penal Colony* and John Cage's

Imaginary Landscape No IV for twelve radios offer the critic different interpretive possibilities.

I believe that all artworks are appropriate objects of interpretation because I believe that all artworks, as Nelson Goodman has argued,[10] characteristically function as symbols. That is, all artworks perform one or another symbolic function: for example, they represent, describe, exemplify, or express. Since interpretive problems can arise with regard to any of these symbolic functions, interpretive problems can arise with regard to any work. For example, even if it were obvious in general what a Grandma Moses or a portrait by Matisse represent, or what a simple lyric describes, it could require interpretation to determine what they exemplify or express. In chapter 7 I discussed one reason why determining what a work expresses may require interpretation. In this chapter I shall discuss others.

I shall not attempt any exhaustive categorization of kinds of critical activities. I shall consider a few questions critics ask about artworks, and thus – since activities will be differentiated in terms of questions asked – a few critical activities. It will emerge that the critic, in attempting to answer any of these questions, can be interpreting. Whether the critic is interpreting on a particular occasion will depend, however, upon other factors as well, for example, what the critic knows$_k$ and what his audience knows$_k$.

Critics characteristically ask of an artwork, 'What is its point?' This question can be understood as a request for either (or both) what the work represents or describes or what the work exemplifies or expresses. I shall illustrate some interpretive possibilities with regard to each of the questions.

When one asks what a picture represents or a passage describes, one can be asking what object, or event, or person the picture or passage literally or metaphorically denotes. For example, when Panofsky asks whether Francesco Maffei's picture of a young woman with a sword in one hand, a charger resting on a beheaded man's head in the other, represents Salome with the head of John the Baptist or Judith with Holofernes,[11] Panofsky could be asking which of these figures (assuming that they were historical persons) were being literally denoted. The interpretive problem here is to determine which of two possible sets of referents is the actual one.

If all images, moreover, are potentially ambiguous – Fantin Latour's *trompe l'oeil* painting *Still Life* is consistent with 'any number of combinations and permutations of real lemons and false flowers, flat or skewy oblique cardboard models of the cup or the book'[12] – and the image becomes unambiguous only in a context, then whenever the context is not known, interpretation is required.

Interpretation can be required even if the subject of an artwork is represented in a straightforward way. For example, determining what an arrested imagine in a photograph represents can present, as Gombrich has shown, an interpretive problem.[13] Given that the image, the record of the light which has entered the lens, does not itself give the viewer information about the distance the light has traveled before it activates the chemical process which results in the image, and given that we cannot tell the size of an object in a picture unless we know its distance from the lens or vice versa, we must sometimes interpret. Interpretation is required, for example, when one does not independently know the object's size and there are no textual clues, etc.

When we turn from the visual arts to the literary arts, we find again that interpretive problems can arise about what works describe or literally denote, about what the passages in them refer to. Given the pervasive ambiguity of a natural language, more than one object or event can be described using the same words, even when the words are not to be taken allegorically, viz., when the words refer to their standard objects. For example, when Hamlet tells Ophelia to 'Get thee to a nunnery', given that 'nunnery' could refer to a place like that which Sweeney finds among the nightingales, or to a place familiar to St Theresa of Avila, we are faced with an interpretive task. Strictly speaking, since *Hamlet* is a fictive work, the interpretive task here would be to find out what kind of description Hamlet's words involved, rather than to find out what was literally described. The phrase in question might easily enough have occurred, however, in a biography written at the time *Hamlet* was written. Our earlier example of 'spare' in Milton's twentieth sonnet would serve here.

When critics are interested in not what is literally denoted but in what is metaphorically denoted, interpretive problems also arise. Consider Eliot's 'broad-backed hippopotamus' and the Church. Hart Crane's 'Immaculate venon binds / the fox's teeth', may refer to the strand of white yarn stretched on the small sharp needles of a knitting or weaving machine.[14] In these cases finding out what the references are can be an interpretive task.

Metaphorical descriptions ('a tattered coat upon a stick') or metaphorical statements ('Life's but a walking shadow') – with which literature is replete – require interpretation. While inviting paraphrase, they are not equivalent to any paraphrase, for metaphors establish new kinds – 'a recess of summer', 'the queen of the rosebud garden of girls' – kinds which have not previously been picked out by any literal classifications.[15]

Questions about a work's point, when understood as questions about what a work exemplifies or expresses, can also require interpretation. For example, if one were to decide in the 'nunnery' example above that the person was ordering the other to a non-religious house, one would still be left with an interpretive question – what do his words express? Is he disgusted or angry or bitter?

Interpretive problems about what a work expresses or exemplifies can arise for a number of reasons. Exemplifying and expressing are interest- or circumstance-relative activities: that is, what a work exemplifies or expresses depends upon the groupings or comparison classes a critic selects for the work. What groupings or comparison classes are selected depends upon the critic's interests, the works that are available to him for the comparison or grouping, the comparisons or groupings that have been standardly made, and so on. Selecting comparison classes can involve interpreting. For example, the critical debate about 'whether *Wuthering Heights* should be read as a perverse fantasy' – as 'laid in hell – only it seems places and people have English names there', or 'as a work of sober realism' – 'about England in 1847',[16] is a debate about which of two comparison classes the work should be put into, which of the two labels 'perverse fantasy work' or 'sober realistic work' does it exemplify?

Which comparison classes are not merely novel but illuminating requires critical deliberation and decision. When George Steiner groups Hegel's parable of 'The master and the servant' with Beckett's *Waiting for Godot*, Genet's *The Maids*, Conrad's *Nostromo*, and Faulkner's novels about Yoknapatawpha county because he believes all of them 'exemplify Hegel's . . . reading of the doomed symbiosis between ruler and subject',[17] he is interpreting these works for his readers.

Artworks do not express or exemplify independently of a context. Given that contexts change – different comparison classes are available to critics at different times – what these works exemplify and express can change. For example, J. M. Turner, if seen in terms of the eighteenth-century ideals of the sublime can be classified as a literary painter – his works have subjects: the sea, darkness, cities, mountains and so on. If one compares him with the abstract color painters of the 1960s, his works may be viewed as early precursors of abstractionism.[18]

If judgements of exemplification and expression were what Frank Sibley has called aesthetic judgements, and if as such they required the exercise of taste – a discriminatory ability that goes beyond normal eyesight, hearing, and intelligence – or if they required, as Hume suggested, discriminatory ability plus sensibility, then it would be apparent why a critic's remark about what is expressed or exemplified is often an interpretive one. Even if the critic could know$_k$ what was expressed or exemplified (assuming absolute precision not to be a requirement), others need not.

Sometimes the interpretive debate about what a work exemplifies or expresses can be the result not of differences in perceptual discrimination or critical understanding but, as Francis Sparshott points out, of differences in taste.[19] Whereas one critic may interpret a work as delicate, another may on the basis of the same first-order discriminations interpret it as effeminate or finicky or timid.

If certain of the classifications critics use (e.g., 'tightly knit', 'deeply moving') were not, as Sibley claims they are not, condition governed in any positive way, then this would suggest why a critic would frequently need to interpret for himself. If it were required (as discussed in chapter 7) that the critical classifications be known to be precisely right, then the critic would always be interpreting for himself as well as for others when he tried to determine what a work expresses.

I have illustrated kinds of critical activity that can count as interpreting. A critic can be interpreting when he attempts to answer questions about representation and description, exemplification and expression. There are other questions critics ask and, therefore, corresponding critical activities. For example, critics may encounter interpretive tasks at a very basic level. They may ask what words are in a text, what colors or shapes in a painting or sculpture. Since artworks often come in different editions (consider, for example, the Quartos and Folio of *Hamlet*), and not all come undamaged (consider the friezes of the Parthenon), a critic may need to interpret in order to determine what words are contained in a text. Has Yorick's skull lain in the earth 'this dozen years' as in the First Quarto, or 'three and twenty years' as in the Quarto of 1604?[20] Likewise, a critic may need to interpret to determine what the shapes or colors of a relief are – we know, for example, that the Greeks painted their marble.

Although questions about what a poem or a play or a painting is might seem philosophers' questions, critics ask and answer them. In doing so, a critic may be interpreting. Moreover, the answer the critic gives to these questions may lead to further interpretation. That is, just as how one interprets dreams will determine what is to count as an interpretation of a dream – consider Freud's interpretation of dreams as wish-fulfillments and the subsequent demand that an interpretation of a particular dream reveal this latent content – so how one interprets a poem, a novel, a painting or a musical composition, will point to the kind of interpretation that is wanted, the kind of thing that would be an interpretation of it. Consider, for example, the myriad things a poem has been interpreted as: 'a system of signs', 'a structure of norms', 'a patterning of intended effects', 'whatever is made of it by a reader'.[21] Moreover, once it has been decided what a poem is, further interpretation may be required. For example, if a poem were interpreted as a system of signs, one would need to decide whether in interpretation it was to be 'reconstructed', 'reconstituted', or 'deconstructed'.

Critics can be interpreting when they attempt to answer questions about the verbal labels critics use. For example, if *Hamlet* is classified as a tragedy (described as one), how is one to understand 'tragedy'? Is one to understand it in terms of emotional purgation, harmartia, tragic flaw?[22] Are the Renaissance masques 'elegant compliments offered to the monarch', or are they 'direct political assertions', 'offered not to him but by him'?[23]

Interpretive questions can also arise about what judgement a critic is making. Suppose a critic says '*Hamlet* is a tragedy about revenge.' How is his remark to be interpreted? Does he mean that the work deals with revenge? If this is what he means, then he is likely to be describing the play. If, however, he is claiming that revenge is the primary concern of the play, then he may be interpreting.[24] Or suppose a critic says Albee's *Tiny Alice* is an obscure play. Does he mean that it is difficult for an average audience to comprehend what the play means, because the play has a hidden meaning or does he mean that the play has a quality of obscurity whether or not it has a hidden meaning?[25]

Although critical interpreting is not a single activity but consists of multiple activities, if my earlier claims are correct, these diverse activities share certain features: the person engaged in them is thinking, is classifying, is able to give reasons for his classifications. If the activity is interpreting for oneself, then the person does not know$_k$, and it is epistemically possible for him to be mistaken about, whether his classifications are correct. If the activity is interpreting for others, then these others do not know$_k$ whether the classifications offered them are correct. In addition I claimed in chapter 8 that the satisfaction of certain conditions was sufficient for interpreting.

If interpreting activities are, as I have suggested, diverse, then one cannot say that critical interpreting in the arts is exclusively like some one kind of interpreting; that is, one cannot say that it is exclusively like interpreting historical events, or natural signs, or motives, or dreams, or passages in philosophical texts, or historical figures, or scores, or scripts, and so on. Some critical interpreting in the arts is like some of these activities, some interpreting is like others. There are, I believe, numerous candidates for illuminating analogies to critical interpretation, not simply the two Stuart Hampshire suggests as illuminating, viz., the interpretation of dreams and the interpretation of the performing artist.[26]

   While I have argued that many of the claims I advance about critical interpreting and interpretation in the arts can be defended independently of one's view about the status of an interpretation, its standard of acceptability, or the character of its object, I have, nevertheless, claimed that while not all interpretations need be statements, nor all interpreting involve stating, a substantial amount of critical interpreting in the arts does involve this. I have also assumed in anti-Derridean fashion that what an artist intended is relevant information if one wants to determine what's in a work, what its point is. However, while I believe it is possible for critics sometimes to show that a work is as the artist intended, or is more like what the artist intended than the artist could have said, I have also claimed that it is possible for critics to show that a work is ways the artist could not or would not have intended, and here I am not referring to failed intentions. As Tom Stoppard suggested, the relationship between an artist and a critic may be akin to that between a customs inspector and a traveller.[27] The inspector opening the traveller's suitcase (the artist's work) finds many things in it which the traveller is forced to acknowledge are in it, although he can truthfully protest that he has not packed them.

Notes

1 Frank Kermode, *The Genesis of Secrecy*, p. 1.
2 Peter Kivy, *The Corded Shell* (Princeton, 1980), p. 53.
3 Kermode, *The Genesis of Secrecy*, p. 1.
4 John Sinclair, in his translation of Dante's *Inferno* (Oxford, 1961), p. 31.
5 Francis Sparshott, *The Concept of Criticism* (Oxford, 1967), pp. 136–7. 'The man most often called an interpreter is the translator, who transposs human messages from unfamiliar languages into familiar ones.' See also Sparshott, *The Theory of the Arts*, p. 249 where he discusses the minor role of the translator interpreter in the arts. 'It may be that the only place for the notion of validity or correctness in criticism in the arts is in connection with the sort of historical exegesis that explains obsolete iconography or

provides glossaries for archaic or dialect terms where in fact, the critical interpreter acts as a translator.'

6 Cf. no. 3, ch. 4.

7 William Empson, *Seven Types of Ambiguity* (London, 1963), p. 114.

8 Mary Sirridge, 'Artistic intentions and critical prerogative', *British Journal of Aesthetics*, 18, no. 2 (Spring 1978), 145, and Joseph Margolis, *Art & Philosophy*, p. 121, limit interpretation to certain objects: Sirridge – '[T]here are artworks which do not require critical interpretation. Paintings which are not allegorical and which are not linked to stories and simple lyric poems are examples of this.' Margolis – 'There is hardly any use in asking for an interpretation, in an aesthetically restricted sense, of a Grandma Moses, a Currier and Ives print, the usual portraits of Matisse, rug designs and the like.'

9 For example, Arthur Danto contends: 'The moment something is considered an artwork, it becomes subject to an *interpretation*. It owes its existence as an artwork to this, and when its claim to art is defeated, it loses its interpretation and becomes a mere thing.' 'Artworks and real things', reprinted in Kennick, *Art and Philosophy* (2nd edn), 108. This quotation taken out of context seems to suggest that only artworks require interpretation – it loses its interpretation – but as Danto makes clear he is not suggesting this. Cf. also Danto's *The Transfiguration of the Commonplace* (Cambridge, 1981), p. 124. Other philosophers have claimed that artworks are essentially ambiguous, there are always 'a range of ways in which the spectator or audience can take a work of art'. (Wollheim, *Art and its Object*, p. 73)

10 Nelson Goodman, 'When is art?', *Ways of World making*, 57–70.

11 Erwin Panofsky, *Studies in Iconology*, p. 12.

12 E. H. Gombrich, *Art and Illusion* (Princeton, 1969) p. 276.

13 E. H. Gombrich, 'Standards of truth: the arrested image and the moving eye', *Critical Inquiry* vol. 7 no. 2 (Winter 1980), 237–73.

14 Martin Staples Shockley, 'Crane's Lachrymae Christi', in *Reading Modern Poetry*, Paul Engle ed., (Chicago, 1955), 323.

15 Nelson Goodman, 'Metaphor as moonlighting', *Critical Inquiry* vol. 6 no. 1 (Autumn 1979), 126–7.

16 Ellen Moers, 'Female Gothic', *New York Review of Books* (4 April 1974), 35.

17 George Steiner, 'Master and man', *New Yorker* (12 July 1982), 102.

18 Hilton Kramer, 'Rare Turner watercolors and prints shown at Yale', *New York Times* (20 February 1981), C1.

19 Sparshott, *The Theory of the Arts*, p. 214.
20 If the First Quarto is taken literally, it suggests Hamlet is nineteen, if the Second Quarto is correct, it suggests Hamlet is thirty.
21 Wayne Booth, *Critical Understanding* (Chicago, 1979), pp. 3–4.
22 Cf. Radford & Minogue, *The Nature of Criticism*, pp. 8–10.
23 Stephen Orgel, *The Illusion of Power* (Berkeley, 1975), p. 52.
24 Radford & Minogue, *The Nature of Criticism*, p. 24.
25 Sparshott, *The Theory of the Arts*, pp. 224–5.
26 Stuart Hampshire, 'Types of interpretation', in Kennick ed., *Art and Philosophy* (2nd edn), 204.
27 Tom Stoppard suggested this in a talk given at Johns Hopkins University.

Index

Abrams, M. H., 96, 97
artworks
  as objects of interpretation, 4
    159–60, 167n
  properties of, 45, 48, 51, 62,
    68–72, 130
Auden, W. H., 85n

Beardsley, Monroe, 5n, 82n
Beckett, Samuel, 81, 109n, 127,
  130, 141n, 148, 163
Booth, Wayne, 168n
Bradbury, Malcolm, 106n
Brecht, Bertolt, 66n, 80
Brueghel, 52, 78, 85n

Carroll, Noel, 142n
Cavell, Stanley, 82n, 83n, 139n
choosing, 155, 156
Cioffi, Frank, 59, 60
Cohen, G. A., 157n
conjecturing, 35, 152, 154, 159
Crews, Frederick, 134–5
critical practice, 1–2, 4, 42–4, 46,
  116, 120–37

Dante, Alighieri, 49–50, 53–4,
  56, 60, 62, 65n, 73
Danto, Arthur, 85n, 167n
deconstruction, 95–105

defeat, significant, 1–2, 90–1,
  94–5, 100, 111, 137
  see also interpretations,
  defeasibility of
de Man, Paul, 63n
De Rougemont, Denis, 69–70
Derrida, Jacques, 4, 5n, 45, 86,
  96–105, 107n, 108n, 109n
describing, 4, 8, 13–14, 144–56,
  160–2
discovery, 3, 4, 45, 68–70, 72
Donoghue, Denis, 140n
Dutton, Denis, 143n

Eliot, T. S., 57, 65n, 66n, 143n,
  162
Empson, William, 74, 167n
exemplifying, 141n, 160, 162–4
experiences-as, reports of, 4,
  35–40, 43, 46, 87–8, 110,
  116–18, 121, 123, 136, 137,
  139n
explaining, 153, 154, 155
expressing, 124–33, 141n, 160,
  162–4

falsifying, 2, 49, 101, 113, 116,
  119, 120–1, 123–4, 133–4
Fish, Stanley, 4, 5n, 45, 84n,